The BRAVEHEARTED GOSPEL

ERIC LUDY

HARVEST HOUSE PUBLISHERS

EUGENE, OREGON

All Scripture quotations are taken from the King James Version of the Bible.

Eric Ludy: Published in association with Loyal Arts Literary Agency, LoyalArts.com.

Cover by Abris, Veneta, Oregon

THE BRAVEHEARTED GOSPEL
Copyright © 2008 by Winston and Brooks, Inc.
Published by Harvest House Publishers
Eugene, Oregon 97402
www.harvesthousepublishers.com

Library of Congress Cataloging-in-Publication Data
Ludy, Eric.
The bravehearted Gospel / Eric Ludy.
   p. cm.
ISBN-13: 978-0-7369-2164-0 (pbk.)
ISBN-10: 0-7369-2164-8 (pbk.)
1. Christianity and culture. I. Title.
BR115.C8L87 2008
243—dc22

2008012049

Printed in the United States of America

08 09 10 11 12 13 14 15 16 / VP-SK / 12 11 10 9 8 7 6 5 4 3 2

I spent five years of my life, starting at the age of 20, praying fervently for what I termed "a father of the faith"—a man who would introduce me to the terrain of the deeper life and inaugurate me into the fellowship of the burning heart. Yet God's answer to my years of tireless prayer merely proved to me His divine sense of humor. For instead of a father, God gave me something altogether unexpected. With a heavenly wink and a curious smile, He gave me Ben, a man four years younger than me.

I can't tell you how many times I have trembled with the sweetest conviction as Ben boomed the truth of Heaven into my soul. I trace my first encounter with many of the epic themes packaged within this book back to a conversation with this Luther-like man. It was Ben who showed me the match and said, "Strike it and set it to the kindling of your soul!" This book is merely the summation of our eight-year friendship. In many ways, it's simply a quotation of Ben's heart and life.

Ben, I know you labor for Heaven's reward alone, but please receive my deepest gratitude. This book is for you. May it always be a reminder that even the hidden years of our lives are not without an effect on this dying world. You have helped beget a man of fire. May I merely be the first of many.

Contents

The Word of a Friend   7

Part One
The Manly Stuff
The bane of a metrosexual society

1   The rather awkward word   17
2   The job no one wants   23
3   Scratching that itch   35
4   Why can't you be more like your sister?   41
5   Blood, dirt, bugs, and mess   45

The Bravehearted Path
Where it begins   51

Part Two
An Ode to Homer
A study in incorrectness and irrelevance

6   Of dying horses and shotguns   59
7   Carl vs. Jane—a losing proposition   63
8   Mean ol' Pastor Carl   69

The Bravehearted Path
The ground rules   75

Part Three
Curb Appeal
Silicone saints and botoxed believers

9   The secret sauce   81
10   Presentation, imitation, and abdication   85
11   Metrotheism   91
12   Dressing up Jesus   95

The Bravehearted Path
Contra mundum   101

Part Four
Mind Wide Open
Standing for nothing, falling for everything

13 Emerging with the truth intact 113
14 Stretching the truth 117
15 The paralysis of infinity 121
16 Wishful thinking is no thinking at all 131
17 Just be real 135
18 Faith or fear—choose your master 141
19 The new atheist and the manly stuff 145
20 The emergent Christian 151

The Bravehearted Path
Living martyrs 153

Part Five
The Bliss of Unknowing
Cultivating ignorance to evade obedience

21 Avoiding truth to become like God 163
22 Eric, the interpreter 169
23 Wikibiblia 171

The Bravehearted Path
The Canon-mind 183

Part Six
The Artful Dodger
Playing Johnnie Cochran with God

24 Miranda 197
25 A face without eyes, a face without tears 203
26 The new legalism 207

The Bravehearted Path
Soli Deo gloria 215

Part Seven
Where do we go from here?
The practical potential of the Bravehearted Gospel

27 Engraced 229

The Bravehearted Path
Epilogue 239
Notes 243

The WORD of a FRIEND

Brown is the new black; emergent is the new Reformation—or at least so some would claim. Like it or not, something new is afoot. After decades of defending the status quo, a cry is now being raised from every quarter, from both young and old alike, for a living, breathing, authentic rendition of the Christian faith that will stoke the fires of the soul, bring back the meaning to life, and revive an ailing church to its very foundations.

In response to this call, something new this way comes. For better or for worse, something is emerging out of the depths of the traditional church. This is not a question; it is a statement of fact. But will this emergent church bring us closer to the truth, as in the Reformation, or lead us further from it?

This book could rightly be labeled *emergent*. It's no great defender of decaying institution, nor is it friend to outmoded and outdated traditions and ritual. And yet, while the rallying cry for drastic change will be heard distinctly within the following pages, it should be noted that the changes being championed between the covers of this book will appear new only to the minds of modern Christians. This seemingly "new" thing of "emerging" from the morass of modern, lukewarm religion is in fact as old as the Roman Empire and as venerable as time itself. The burning heart of the ancient faith must once again come to beat in the breast of Christ's followers in the twenty-first century, or all is lost.

The truths shouted from every paragraph you are about to read only sound new but they are not. They are certainly *emergent* in relation to the modern church, but they are undoubtedly *historic* in regards to the foundations of Christianity.

It is true we must emerge from the ghetto of religion or we die. But we must emerge with historical Christianity intact, or we will have saved our life only to lose it in the end.

Eric has written an unflinchingly "historic emergent" book. With sometimes ruthless intensity and a pen that often cuts as deeply as a sword, he sets about the thankless task of scraping off the barnacles of error that over time have attached themselves to the truth; while with equal fervor he defends the ancient faith that was once and for all delivered to the saints, refusing to throw the baby out with the barnacles.

Keep this in mind as you read. The radical "new" stance being pressed with both clarity and passion in the upcoming chapters is not some newfangled theological novelty but is rooted and grounded in none other than the life, teachings, and example of Jesus Christ.

I guess that brings up an important question: What *was* Jesus like?

After all, if He is the historic example of everything that we are to be at this very moment in time, then what was He like?

If we could, just for a moment, emerge from our cocoon of political and religious correctness, and if we would be willing to lay down all prejudice and preconceived notions and stare the historic man Himself in the face, the results might be so shockingly foreign to our minds that we may find this historic Jesus emerging as unrecognizable to our modern Christian sensibilities; and all this, not because we invented something new, but because we returned to something old.

Most of us have heard that God is love, that God became flesh, and that Jesus was His name. However, it is a stunning truth that it is not enough to merely say that Jesus was loving, or that He was loved, or even that He knew how to love. Jesus *was* love, He was the very essence of the stuff, bound up in blood, bone, and sinew; He was love walking on two feet, breathing the dusty air of Judea, living to give life to men.

Jesus was perfect, and He lived the only perfect life that's ever been lived. These words are well-worn and have been repeated more times than can be numbered. But do we realize the practical implications of such a statement? It means that in all things, and at all times, Jesus was perfectly loving, perfectly unselfish, and perfectly humble. He was perfectly righteous, and perfectly holy. In fact He was perfect in every way. The Bible says that He was without sin. Jesus was blameless. Not once in His life was He ever arrogant, boastful, or proud. The number of times that Jesus spoke an unkind word or mindlessly lashed out with His tongue came to a grand total of zero. He had no blind spots. His doctrine was pure. He never erred in His teaching by placing an over- or underemphasis on any doctrine. He never spoke out of prejudice, mere opinion, or dogma. He transcended His culture. He spoke only what His Father gave Him to speak, and His words were the words of God. He came to serve others, not to be served Himself. He made no attempt to manipulate the masses for His own gain, but lived humbly and without pretension. He was approachable. Women, children, tax collectors, prostitutes, and even lepers came to Jesus and were never turned away. He taught that we should love one another, that we should treat others as we ourselves would like to be treated, and that we should do good even to those who use and mistreat us.

And yet this perfect man of love was viciously and brutally killed by a mob, spitting hatred and cursing His name.

How is this possible? Why did it happen?

If we would know the whole of the story and not only half, then we must acknowledge that the historical Jesus was not *just* love in the flesh, He was also truth in the flesh and He was born into a world that loved lies. Jesus said, "I *am* the truth." You see, it's not that Jesus was merely truthful, or that He knew the truth, or even that He taught the truth. Jesus *was* the truth—He was the very essence of the stuff. He was truth walking on two feet and living to set men free.

We like love. Love deals in relationships, while truth deals in cold hard facts. But Jesus never compromised one for the other.

The problem we have with truth is that it cares nothing for our feelings or preferences, and pays no tribute to our opinions or the sacredness of our dogma. Truth is about reality. It is concerned not with the way we believe things to be, or the way we would like them to be, but with the way things actually are. Truth is spun from the fabric of facts and therefore cannot bend to accommodate the wishes or sensibilities of the masses. Truth is not the product of a vote or a democracy and has nothing to do with the will of the people. It will not bow to the wealthy like a preening politician. It cannot be bribed. Nor can it, in the name of compassion, make exception for the aged or the unfortunate. It never has and never will enter into agreement with the proud or unbelieving and offers no parley to the religious and the self-righteous. Truth is what it is.

Regardless of the opinions, feelings, preferences or historical and cultural contexts of billions of people, the Earth *is* round. There is simply nothing that can be done with this, or any other truth, but yield to, acknowledge, and accept it. That's really all we can do with the truth. And that is why men, for the most part, hate it. As humans, we tend to despise the things we have no power or control over, the things we cannot manipulate or steer toward our own ends and purposes. How much more, then, do we often find ourselves railing against God's truth, which not only obstinately refuses to cater to our agendas but, quite to the contrary, adamantly claims that we should become its servant?

I don't know if there is a person in the Western world who hasn't heard the following words:

> God so loved the world, that he gave his only begotten Son (John 3:16).

That has to be the most famous verse in the Bible. And who wouldn't love a verse that so clearly articulates the love of God toward fallen man? But the forgotten stepchild to this text is the one that follows three verses later—the one that describes humanity's reaction to their God's amazing generosity:

> Light is come into the world, and men loved darkness rather than light, because their deeds were evil (verse 19).

Just because Light took on flesh and was given to this world in love does not mean that He ceased to be Light. Jesus said, "I *am* the light of the world." You see, it's not that Jesus simply had light, or that He walked in the light, or even that He pointed to the light. Jesus *was* the Light, He was the very essence of the stuff, piercing, with painful intensity, a world enamored with darkness. He was light walking on two feet upon the storm-tossed waters of Galilee, living to give sight to men.

There is simply no other way to say it: light is a reproof to darkness, truth is a rebuke to lies, and Christ, who was literally love with skin on, in so many ways was a rebuke to our rebel race.

This is why He was murdered.

The historical Jesus was not crucified because *God so loved the world.* No! The only begotten of the Father was fastened with iron nails to an unforgiving cross because He spoke the truth with authority and glistened with the light of heaven *and men loved darkness rather than light.*

So what am I getting at?

If Jesus, who was perfect, who never sinned, and who was love incarnate, could not speak the truth without being hated, rejected, and despised, who are we to think that we can do better? Who are we to think that we have figured out a more "loving" and "relevant" way to present the truth in a more "seeker-friendly" manner than Jesus Christ, the Son of God?

We have wholeheartedly embraced the sentimental, watercolor Jesus that seems to spend most of His time holding lambs and patting children on the head with some faraway, glazed-over, dreamy look in His eye. And we tend to shy away from, or altogether ignore, that man who spoke the truth of God so boldly that conspiracies were hatched, witnesses were bribed, and politicians were entreated to bring about His painful and public execution.

What do we do with this? What do we do with that side of Christ's message that brings about such a violent response from the culture and quite often from the church itself? What do we do with that Christ who puts down the lamb, mounts the temple steps with whip clenched in white-knuckled fist, and insists, as He turns over the tables of the money changers, that when it was written "My house shall be called a house of prayer" it was not a suggestion that was to be interpreted in the historical context of the culture to which it was first written, but that it was the eternal command and declaration of the will of almighty God and it was to be obeyed?

What do we do with this Jesus?

We use clichés like, "Well, we have to speak the truth in love," as if speaking the truth in love will somehow change the truth and the world's reaction to it—as if light and darkness will somehow get along, if only the light would speak in "love." Jesus spoke the truth in love like no one who has ever lived, and the world hated Him just the same because He dared to speak the truth at all.

What about you and me? Are we the exception? Do we know something that Jesus Himself didn't know? The world hasn't changed and truth hasn't changed. So why is the church, the bride of Christ, trying so hard to get in bed with what the Bible defines as God's sworn enemy?

Why *do* we get along so well with the world when Jesus, the most loving being who ever breathed air, was sent to an early grave by the same social system that we're trying to make peace with? Could it be that we are trying to imitate only half a Savior, attempting to bring only His love to the world without boldly illuminating it with His truth?

> This is not the way of Christ.
>
> This is not the way of His disciples.
>
> This is not the the bravehearted path.

Now, all of this could conveniently remain a mere intellectually stimulating exercise if not for the fact that just before His death, at the hands of a light-despising mob, Jesus looked down through time and called each and every one of us to follow Him. And to those who would heed the call of their Lord He gave these promises:

> "The servant is not greater than his lord" (John 13:16).
>
> "If the world hates you, know that it hated me before it hated you" (John 15:18).
>
> "Be of good cheer; I have overcome the world" (John 16:33).

In the early days of the first century A.D., 12 men picked up this gauntlet when thousands of others shook their heads and walked away. They followed their Master fully. They loved the lost with His passion, they spoke the truth with His thunder, and though often persecuted and oppressed, their lives sparkled with His light. Almost every one of them, within a few decades, had followed Jesus to their deaths at the hands of a world that still loved darkness rather than light. But their sacrifice was not in vain, and by the time the last apostle had breathed his final breath, it was commonly said, "These [were the men who] turned the world upside down" (Acts 17:6).

Twelve against the world.

Twelve who chose the gritty bravehearted path.

Twelve was enough.

May it be so today.

The book you hold in your hands is a catalyst for revolution, latent with the truth of God, burning with the light of Heaven, and beating with the same holy love that coursed through martyrs' veins. The truth between its covers, like the cross, is often neither comfortable nor pretty. But, like the cross, it is salvation to those who will dare to look it full in the face.

This book doesn't flinch to the left or the right in an effort to avoid the sticky issues, but neither is it unloving or unkind. The light of another world dusts its edges and gilds its pages, illuminating a path trod by the greatest men and women in history—the path of the Bravehearted Gospel. To many, at first glance, this path seems too hard, too straight, or too narrow. But I encourage you to press on, for the testimony of those who have walked this sacred corridor before us is that its fruit is sweet, its air is clean, its company is unequaled, and its destination is unmatched—and all this with the smile of God warm upon the soul.

So press on to the mark! Lay hold of the prize! The King has called. Who will answer? The race has been set. Who will run? The bravehearted path is the path of our Master; it is a way of thorns and it is a road of glory, and those who run it must run it with all their might.

I wish you Godspeed.

Ben Davenport
COFOUNDER OF THE STONE MOUNTAIN PROJECT

Part One

THE MANLY STUFF

The bane of a metrosexual society

One

THE RATHER AWKWARD WORD

One of my least favorite words in the English language is *castrate*. It is a rather awkward word denoting a rather awkward thing. And for better or worse, it's a word not typically allowed into a Christian book. And I, for one, am the happier for it. In fact, I can think of no worse way to spend my leisure reading time than to be laboring through a book that repeatedly used such a distasteful word. I'm sure we can all agree that such an unpleasant word belongs in historical reference books on ancient Siam and not in essays on the grand and holy adventure of Christianity.

That said, I wish to make us all a little uncomfortable. I plan to do in the third paragraph of this book what could spell this book's doom. I am going to not just use this unseemly word but I am going to define it. I realize the cost of such a maneuver. But when you understand how significant this unpleasant word is in light of the topic of this book, I think you will realize why I have no option but to push forward.

Castrate: to surgically remove a man's input, potency; his force; his influence; and his strength. (Note: you can thank me later for not giving you the scientific definition.)

I realize that you are probably standing in a bookstore at this moment, previewing this book and wondering if you should buy it. Your friend probably said something like, "You really need to read this book." But you are thinking to yourself right now, "My friend didn't mention anything about *this!*" But please know that this supremely uncomfortable word, now that it has been defined, has almost officially served its purpose in this book and will be seen only twice more.

As far as words go, I will readily agree that the word *castrate* is both ugly and unpoetic. Not many songwriters are going to stick it into their lyrics, and not many poets are pining to find the perfect rhyme for it in order to jam it onto the end of their prose. So I'm not going to try and pitch it to you as a word to implement into your vocabulary turnstile. Simply put, there are just no more refined and flowery words that can substitute for it. *Emasculate* is by far the closest word to fit the bill, and therefore, I will resort to plugging it in as a more noble substitute throughout the pages of this book. However, *emasculate* has a softer, more disarming feel and therefore can't possibly fully replace the much-needed shock and alarm that oozes out of the word chosen to begin this book.

And as hard as I've tried to think of a better way to lay the groundwork for what this book is all about, I keep coming back to this crazy, ugly word. It says it clearly and concisely, though it may say it with a little too much flamboyance. You see, I believe that the "manly stuff" has been unconsciously removed from the body of Christ today. We are missing the manly input, potency, force, influence, and strength in Christ's body. Some may feel uncomfortable that Jesus was a man, but there is no way around the fact that He was. And yet His body, the church, is strangely lacking the evidence of this fact in our modern Christian world. Jesus has suddenly gone metrosexual in America. He's male, but He's a male that seems ashamed of His masculinity.

Everyone seems to have an opinion about how this book should be written.

"Eric, I like you, so I'm going to give it to you straight. You have to be careful not to come across like one of those Fundamentalist types!"

"You can't sound too preachy; otherwise, people will just slam the book shut!"

"You better not say it the way you just said it to me, or else people will be doing book burnings with this thing!"

"Oh, and Eric, just have fun when you write this!"

The goal of every book is to not just be written, but read. There are many ways in which this book could have been written, but few that would lend it that much-needed magnetic charm inherent in every truly engaging read. You see, this book is about uncomfortable things. And, I must admit, uncomfortable things are much more difficult to write about than ideas that scratch the back and massage the ego.

Whereas this book has loads of magnetic charm *to me*, I honestly don't know if others will feel the same charm as they venture through its rough terrain. You, dear reader, must decide if I handled this topic well. For I'm certain you will have an opinion in the matter. There will be those who will criticize me for being too soft as well as those who will consider pressing criminal charges against me for being too hard. Frankly, my goal is to handle this topic with the loving dexterity of Jesus Christ.

I wrote this book because I had to. I just couldn't hold it in any longer.

I sat down in front of my laptop on June 4, 2007, with the intent of writing a completely different book. I stared at my computer screen for two straight days and agonized over the reality that God was pointing at something different. I'll never forget the conversation I had with Leslie, my wife, as I shared with her the burning compulsion to write a book about the Bravehearted Gospel.

"You have to write this!" she said pointedly in response. "And when you do, you need to write it like a man!"

So please know it was none other than a sweet, ultrafeminine girly girl, named Leslie, who infused the necessary steel into my spine to actually do this. Whereas the irony of that might not be fully appreciated at this moment, it is certainly still worthy of being mentioned here.

You see, this book has *boy* scribbled all over it. To paraphrase Alan Marshall Beck, this book is "Truth with dirt on its face, Beauty with a cut on its finger, Wisdom with bubble gum in its hair, and the Hope of the future with a frog in its pocket." But don't be fooled into thinking that this is a book about manhood. This is a truth book, and I would like to think that truth books can cross the gender barrier, even though they may speak in a man's tone, with a man's zeal, and a man's grit.

The manly voice has been separated from truth for far too long and so, even at risk of speaking too loudly and too brashly inside the hushed church sanctuary, this book is going to inject a serious amount of muscle back into the gospel life.

Girls, I'm going to say this up front because I wish to be perfectly clear on this point: This book may very well sound like the tribal war cries of a bunch of painted men, but it is not a man book. The truth of the Bravehearted Gospel is without equivocation a truth that *must* be adopted into the feminine heart. As much as a great man must learn to listen, cry, be sympathetic, and allow compassion to ebb in his being, so a great woman must have a brave heart. She must have the grit, the growl, and the gusto of God drilled into the bedrock of her soul.

This message is literally burning a hole in my soul. It is everything the modern church is needing and not realizing it needs. It is historic Christianity brought back to life, an invigoration of that ancient power and potency that once steered the early church.

Like many of you, I've grown up amidst a sterile, weak, North American church. We talk a good talk, but when it comes down to living it out in the real world, we're nearly impotent. We talk about love, joy, peace, victory, and blessed happiness, but few in our ranks actually exhibit these basic evidences of the Christian faith. And what is disconcerting, is the fact that even fewer within the church show concern over this gross hypocrisy in our global presentation of Jesus Christ. As a group, we Christians are soft, mushy, and lax. There seems to be a serious shortage of the majestic, intrepid, daring, just, and durable qualities the church once possessed. The steel of a man is strangely lacking.

For instance: Whatever happened to the idea of sacred honor, unvarnished nobility, and unwavering allegiance to the King? What happened to the quake-in-my-boots fear of God, the lay-it-all-on-the-line commitment to the cause of Christ, and the die-if-I-must attitude toward defending truth and Scripture? Where did the radical abandon to seek and save the lost disappear to, or the once glorious idea of martyrdom? Or how about the burning need to stand against evil, to break the jaws of the wicked in order to ransom the oppressed, the orphaned, the widowed, and the enslaved? Where is the holy boldness, the courage, and the daring needed to birth the truth of Christ into this God-forsaking culture? What happened to the once noble idea of preaching with both authority and conviction? Where has the vanguard, the mighty men, the fiercely loyal regiment of King Jesus vanished to? Because we need them, and we need them now!

You see, the Bravehearted Gospel is not merely a title, it is an attitude and a lifestyle. It isn't something I invented. Rather, it comes straight out of the soldier's handbook from Heaven, covered in blood, sweat, tears, and glory. And if I may be so bold, the Bravehearted Gospel is the manly stuff that the modern church is missing, and if it were to be found again, this world might be turned upside down within a single year.

The Bravehearted Gospel is gritty living, the stuff of martyrs and saints. Its bravado meets brains; its hamlike fist meets poetlike heart; its forehead of flint meets tender, love-inspired soul. The Bravehearted Gospel is muscular zeal meets helpless orphan, sacrificing life and limb to rescue her. It is spine of steel bending to embrace the urine-stained outcast, giving up everything in order to see him brought through Heaven's gates. The Bravehearted Gospel is not mushy logic, it is concrete truth. It's not postmodern or modernistic thinking, and it's not dry-as-dust tradition for tradition's sake. Rather, it is historical living ripped straight from the pages of Scripture and made incarnate in the lives of the disciples of Jesus in this twenty-first century. The Bravehearted Gospel isn't soft with sin and it's not hard on sinners, but rather it is the giving up of everything to see sin trumped and the sinner rescued. The Bravehearted Gospel is pure adventure, a life of nuclear joy and hallowed ecstasy. It's the hard way to live, and yet the most satisfying. And, God patiently waits to once again infuse the potency of His Bravehearted Gospel back into the bloodstream of the body of Christ. Ironically, it is you and me, and a million other Christians who are often standing in the way.

Now, I want to let you in on a few things.

First, one of the themes you'll stumble across throughout this book is the concept of nobility. In light of this, I am going to use the old King James translation and its majestic, poetic, and high tone whenever I quote Scripture throughout the upcoming pages. For those of you, like me, who have grown up on the newer translations of the Bible, I think you will find it to be an enchanting, graceful, and refreshing take on ideas that otherwise may have grown a bit stale. Yes, it's a more difficult translation, but when you get past its strong cologne, I think you will find, as I have, that it speaks with a lionlike voice.

Second, in all my previous ten books, I have made the disclaimer that names have been changed to protect individuals' identities. However, in this book, whereas that is true for almost every name used, there are a few names that I will say plainly without veil. I have contemplated this move for quite some time. But I feel that, in this case, it is necessary to help you, as the reader, better understand the specifics of what the modern church is facing. When everyone speaks in generalities often everyone agrees, but true change and true illumination often demands specifics. I pray to God that whenever I do choose to be specific in naming an individual in this book that my thoughts will be offered with the utmost respect and presented with humility and grace.

Also, at the conclusion of each of the seven sections of this book you will find a special chapter entitled "The Bravehearted Path." It is here that the manly stuff becomes practical and real. And it is here that I will give you peeks into what this extraordinary idea of the Bravehearted Gospel is all about. To understand the Bravehearted Gospel, you have to understand the mind, the heart, and the attitude behind it. And because we, as the modern church, have strayed quite far from our historic moorings, we consequently have a long way to go in order to get back to the grand and stately bearing of bravehearted christianity. I hope and pray that this humble literary offering will play a role, by God's grace, to help lead us home.

I'm a man in the defining season of my life. There are males, and there are men. I beg God daily to be counted among the men. But, even as one of the men, there are multiple grades of honor a man can achieve throughout his life. And I must admit that I am still at the lowest rungs. I have merely begun this journey and in no way do I yet deserve to be associated with the noble idea of the Bravehearted Gospel, let alone have my name on the cover of a book associated with such a regal idea.

But there is one thing I possess that allows me to enter these sacred halls and speak about these lofty and princely ideas—*hunger.* I hunger for these truths more than I yearn for anything else. I esteem them; I passionately desire them; and I want them planted into the bedrock of my soul and integrated into the fabric of my being, no matter the pain and no matter the cost.

If I were to write this book ten years from now, I'm sure I would write it differently, and I'm sure there would be things I would add and things I would remove. For all those things that I should have added, forgive me. And for all those things I should have removed, please kindly try and overlook them.

I pray this book will serve to acquaint you, in a more intimate way than you ever thought possible, with the great power and great love of our King Jesus. This book isn't about me, so I pray you look away if ever it seems like Eric Ludy is poking his head up too high within the text. This book is about Jesus, for Jesus, and to Jesus. And as Luke wrote unto Theophilus, so now I write unto my precious King.

Two

THE JOB NO ONE WANTS

It's considered by many that the book of Job is the oldest book of the Bible. Whether it was written before the time of Moses no one knows, but the story itself seems to have taken place long before Moses' era. Anyone who has spent time studying the book of Job knows that whereas it is a profound declaration of God's power and glory, it is also a rather uncomfortable book to read. Why?

Because we are all afraid of being Job.

Just listen to the beginning of this story:

> The LORD said unto Satan, Whence comest thou? Then Satan answered the LORD, and said, From going to and fro in the earth, and from walking up and down in it. And the LORD said unto Satan, Hast thou considered my servant Job, that there is none like him in the earth, a perfect and an upright man, one that feareth God, and escheweth evil?[1]

Now, why in the world God is spending even a moment of His time bantering about with Satan is one of the befuddling things about this story. However, what usually grips our attentions is this whole notion, "Hast thou considered my servant Job?" That could easily read, "Hast thou considered my servant Eric?" or "Hast thou considered my servant (insert your name here!)?"

It's funny, but whereas most of us would love to be noticed by God, applauded by God, and selected by God for the most important tasks, there is a very large part of us that does not want God bringing up our name in conversation—especially with Satan, the enemy of our souls.

After all, for those of us familiar with the story, Job goes on to lose everything—his children, his estate, his livestock, his health, and his dignity—all because of this crazy conversation that, in all of our minds, was ill-conceived on God's part in the first place.

Long and short, there is hardly a one of us on planet Earth who wishes to be Job. Sure, he sounds like a wonderful man, but most of us are willing to forgo the "wonderful" description to avoid the misery that this man incurred.

I have spent a lot of time thinking, studying, and praying about this man's life. I recognize that there is a part of me that wishes to back away from being made available to God in such a manner. There is a part of me that wishes to remain anonymous in Hell. There is a part of me that just utterly resists the notion of publishing my address on Satan's bulletin board with a message that reads, "Bring it!"

But this cowardly part of me is growing lesser and lesser with every passing month. And there is another part of me that is awakening, finding its legs, and discovering its growl. There is an ever-increasing bravehearted part of me that is wanting precisely what Job had.

In fact, if I could say it succinctly, *I want to be just like Job.*

Don't get me wrong, I'm not wishing for the enemy to have unhindered access to my children, my estate, my livestock, my health, and my dignity. But I am wishing for my all-powerful God to have unrestricted license to do with my children, my estate, my livestock, my health, and my dignity anything that He deems fit—*for His glory!*

The book of Job is a book about God's glory. We always look at it as a book about an abused man. But this whole drama isn't about a man. Rather, it is about this man's God.

Satan had tarnished both God's glory and His honor.

Satan was seeking to undermine the faith of the inhabitants of Heaven in their Sovereign King.

Right there, at the beginning of the book, Satan claims that followers of God, such as Job, follow Him only out of lust and not love. Before all the hosts of Heaven Satan threw down the gauntlet, saying that God's servants serve Him only because God bribes them with health, wealth, and prosperity, thus implying that God was not loved as a benevolent master but was rather little more than a well-to-do dictator who bought the favor of His subjects with His coin.

Who would answer this challenge? Who would rise to the occasion and wipe the spit from off God's face?

The answer is Job.

After all, who else could do it? Job *was* the subject in question. *Did* he serve God for love? Or did he serve for profit?

"Remove Your protection from him and he will curse You to Your face!" Satan screamed.

But God knew Job. He knew His servant. And He knew the stuff that Job was made of.

"Everything he has and everything he is I will place within your hands," God replied. "But you are wrong. Job is perfect. And he is upright in all his ways. And though you bring all the weight of the world down like a hammer upon him, he will shun evil and he will choose good. You will fail. And he *will* defeat you."

God wagered His entire reputation on the faithfulness of one man. That man was Job.

And *he* was God's champion.

The grandstands of Heaven must have hushed with the awe of holy angels as they silently watched while Satan, the Prince of the principalities and the powers of the air, brought his worst against tiny Job, God's lone defender in this cosmic conflict.

Those watchers from the portals of glory must have leaned forward with anxious expectation as the end of round one was called. Job's estate lay in ruins, his livestock were gone, his wealth was taken, and his children were dead. Satan stood back, panting and winded with effort as he waited to hear the doubt-filled cry of outrage and angst that *must* issue forth against God from the soul of a man who has suffered the loss of so much within the space of so few hours.

But to the grinding of Satan's teeth and to Heaven's everlasting joy, the Bible records that Job, God's man—though beaten and bloody, though vexed and tempted to curse God and die—fell down upon the ground and *worshiped* God, saying, "Naked came I out of my mother's womb, and naked shall I return thither: the LORD gave, and the LORD hath taken away; blessed be the name of the LORD."[2]

The shouting in heaven must have sounded like peals of thunder.

Not only had Job valiantly taken everything that Satan threw at him and not *cursed* God, but Job had actually *blessed* Him!

To many an onlooker, Job may have seemed to have been struck down without cause. But in reality it was Job who had struck a major blow against Satan and against his lies about God and about God's children.

With no small grief, God had allowed this man to be spent, without him even knowing why, so that both Heaven and Earth *would* know with certainty, from the moment of Job's triumph over Satan unto the end of the ages, that God is no dictator, and that His servants serve Him for love's sake and for love's sake alone.

Down through the years, many have looked upon Job's suffering with wagging heads and called it pointless. But Heaven knows better.

Job was Heaven's champion.

Job stood when everything in him wanted to fall.

Job was a living martyr.

Job had the manly stuff.

Do we?

Could our God lean as heavily upon us? Could we be trusted with such a sacred task as defending the honor of God? Are there those among us of whom God could say, "Satan, you may do your worst but he will not bend; you may bring in your biggest guns but she will not break; they have built their house upon a rock and they shall not be moved. They shall run and not grow weary; they shall walk and not faint. For I know them. They are my sons, they are my daughters, they are my servants, and they will not fail me"?

This is the stuff that changes the world. This is the stuff of the Bravehearted Gospel.

And if Abraham was the father of the faith, then Job was the father of the stalwart heart that would not bend in the heat of battle.

The book of Job opens with this line:

> There was a man in the land of Uz, whose name was Job; and
> that man was perfect and upright, and one that feared God,
> and [shunned][3] evil.

There are a few things I would like to mention about this opening line. First, "the land of Uz"—what a bizarre place! But what's interesting about it is that *Uz* means "a place of wood." Second, the name *Job* means, "hated and despised." Can you imagine Job as an infant being held soothingly in his mother's arms as she whispers sweetly to her husband, "Let's name him Job, honey!"?

The whole book seems strange and a tad bewildering until we realize what it links us to. Where else in the Bible do *wood* and someone *hated and despised* get put together in one story? That's right—the despised King who bore our shame and our penalty upon the wood. And the same thing could be said about Jesus as is always said about Job: "Oh, I'd hate to be that guy!"

But the essence of the Christian life is to not *just know* this Jesus, but to become *like* Him, to bear His shame, to carry His purpose, to share in His sufferings, and to be a bearer of His glory!

When we are first born into the Christian life, our spirits are awakened and the infantile cry of our soul is, "I see, I breathe, I believe!" God holds us soothingly in His fatherly arms and whispers sweetly to Jesus, His Son, "Let's name him Job!"

We are all called to be "a man in the land of Uz, whose name was Job." We are all called to pick up the shameful beams of wood and walk the long, dusty road to the cross as the "hated and despised" in this world. We are called just as our King was called.

I realize that there is a part of you, as I proclaim this, that is scurrying about looking for a "Johnnie Cochran" loophole. But Jesus left us none. He said, "Unless you take up your cross and follow Me, you *cannot* be My disciple." There is a part of every one of us that sees the "wood" and sees the name *Job* and desperately desires to distance ourselves from it. And it is the very same part of us that wants to run and hide when our Messiah is lifted up on two beams of wood and is mocked, ridiculed, spat upon, and crucified. But Jesus also said, "Whosoever therefore shall confess me before men, him will I confess also before my Father which is in heaven."[4]

My sister, Krissy, once said to me, "Eric, the truest test of love and allegiance is found at the cross. Just imagine that you are standing at the crucifixion scene. An angry mob is hollering spiteful invectives at your Lord, falsely accusing Him, denigrating His person. What would you do? True love and allegiance would rouse itself to walk to the foot of His cross, turn toward the crowd, and with trembling finger pointed upward, toward that bloody, naked, pulp of a man, and yell out, 'I'm with Him!'"

Job wasn't a miserable man, and neither was Jesus. Sure, they were both men of sorrows, but they were also men of overwhelming joy. Read the book of Job afresh and you will realize that the overall tenor of Job's life wasn't misery, but incalculable blessing. The story in that book covers the passage of just over a week in Job's life. A week! Likewise, Jesus is not a depressed character. He is not a "woe is Me" sort of fellow—quite to the contrary, He is the Prince of Peace, Love itself, the Fullness of Joy, Radical Triumph, and the Blessing of Heaven.

Jesus was despised by this world, but He was approved of God. And though He carried the misery of the world on His strong and able shoulders during those last days leading up to His death nearly 2000 years ago, at the close of *His* week of misery, He rose again to new life, the Victor!

We are called to follow the Job–Jesus pattern.

Both Job and Jesus were righteous men who suffered not for their own sins, but as God's champions in the battle of the ages, carrying out God's purposes at great personal cost, so that through it all, the name of God might be glorified.

And now *we* are being asked to rise up and follow in the footsteps of these two great men, as well as untold thousands of others who have braved jungles and mountains and deserts for the salvation of the lost and for the glory of their King. We are being called to follow the hallowed track of these men and women who, like Jesus and Job, have suffered the loss of all things for the fame of their Father. We are being asked to lay down our lives that the life of God might be made evident to this dying world. We are asked to yield up our bodies that the strength of God might be seen by dying men. And we are asked to relinquish our every possession into God's keeping that the glory of God might be made manifest in all of its fullness, power, and life.

The bravehearted life, the life of Job, the life of Jesus, is nothing less than the handing over of the keys to our possessions, our soul, and our future to God and saying, "For whatever it's worth, this whole outfit from top to bottom, from left to right, from here to there, inside and out, the whole kit-n-caboodle is yours to do with and to spend as you see fit." It's offering not just the scraps but the whole of our very existence to our God-King and saying, "I know that there's not much here to work with. But please, take it, break it, multiply it, and feed the hungry. And whether by pain or by comfort, whether by sorrow or by joy, whether by life or by my death, glorify Thy name in all the earth!"

Although the road may at times be rocky, and often uphill, the life lived on the straight and narrow bravehearted path is still the greatest road any man or woman could ever hope to walk. As is mentioned in the beginning of this book (based on Ben's foreword), we are being called into a life in which the fruit is sweet, the air clean, the company unequaled, and the destination unmatched—and all this with the smile of God warm upon the soul.

I want to be like Job. I want to be like Jesus. I want my life to be known in both Heaven and in Hell. By the grace of my God, I wish to be such a man that my King would bring me up in conversation and choose me as the vehicle through which He will bring forth His glory, even if at great cost to myself.

It's amazing, but there is no one other than Jesus in Scripture that is associated, morally, with the word *perfect* except Job.[5] Who is this guy anyway? *Perfect* is an awfully strong word. *Upright* is also a rare word used to describe a man in the Bible. Throughout Scripture, the idea of *right*eousness is spared for the Messiah and little else. In other words, this guy had something rare, and whatever he had, I say let's go after it as hungry lions do an evasive wildebeest.

But what made Job so special that the holy God of Heaven singled him out from all the people on the planet as His champion?

The church, for the most part, has spent so much time avoiding this guy because of how uncomfortable his one week of suffering makes us feel that we have forgotten to ask about the decades of life that Job lived in a way that was so pleasing to God that He boasted to Satan about his upright and perfect example.

What was it about Job's life that was so amazing that even God was impressed?

Well, if you start paging through the book of Job, you eventually come to a chapter in which Job himself tells of this life which God described as perfect and upright.

I happen to have developed quite an affinity for this particular chapter. Not only does it possess the grit and the growl of the Christ-life, but it also is richly laden with the love and compassion of God's kingdom. It's the Bravehearted Gospel pure and simple. It's the bravehearted life, the bravehearted manner, the bravehearted voice, and the bravehearted attitude. This twenty-ninth chapter of Job is where the Bravehearted Gospel was first birthed into my heart and mind. This is the manly stuff not only of Job, but of Jesus. And it powerfully represents the type of masculine emphasis that is supposed to be inherent in both the men and women of the church triumphant. This is a description of the life of Job, the perfect and upright man. This is what Christ's body is supposed to look and function like.

So, why am I making such a big deal out of Job's life and about the twenty-ninth chapter of his book?

I don't know. I guess it's just that when God points to something and calls it perfect, we should probably pay attention.

When I read Job 29, I perspire. It moves me. It takes the match of the Spirit of God and strikes it within my soul, and sets me aflame. It's everything I want, everything I desire in my life. I want to take those words and somehow mainline them directly into the jugular of my existence. I wish to live them, animate them, pronounce them in moving human form once again on planet Earth.

This book isn't intended to be a detailed exegesis on Job 29, but merely an extension of its sacred and inspiring substance. But still, let me give you a little peek into this chapter's grandeur and majesty. Now I have shortened it slightly, but here is Job describing his life—the life that impressed the God of the universe:

> Oh that I were as in months past, as in the days when God preserved me; when his candle shined upon my head, and when by his light I walked through darkness…when the Almighty was yet with me…
>
> When I went out to the gate through the city, when I prepared my seat in the street! The young men saw me, and hid themselves: and the aged arose, and stood up. The princes refrained talking, and laid their hand on their mouth. The nobles held their peace, and their tongue cleaved to the roof of their mouth. When the ear heard me, then it blessed me; and when the eye saw me, it gave witness to me: Because I delivered the poor that cried, and the fatherless, and him that had none to help him. The blessing of him that was ready to perish came upon me: and I caused the widow's heart to sing for joy. I put on

righteousness, and it clothed me: my judgment was as a robe and a diadem. I was eyes to the blind, and feet was I to the lame. I was a father to the poor: and the cause which I knew not I searched out. And I brake the jaws of the wicked, and plucked the spoil out of his teeth...

My root was spread out by the waters, and the dew lay all night upon my branch. My glory was fresh in me, and my bow was renewed in my hand.

Unto me men gave ear, and waited, and kept silence at my counsel. After my words they spoke not again and my speech dropped upon them. And they waited for me as for the rain; and they opened their mouth wide as for the latter rain...I chose out their way, and sat chief, and dwelt as a king in the army, as one that comforts the mourners.

You'll notice within the very first sentence of the text that Job wasn't a mere legalist simply fulfilling his moral duties. He was a man who navigated his way through the darkness of this world and lived his life by the very light of God. Job wasn't a loner living out some dead, dutiful religion, for the passage says that God was *with* him. This man had a living relationship with the King of kings.

Like Jesus, Job was a possessor of great wealth and power. And like Jesus, Job apparently left suburbia to spend both himself and his vast resources on the weak and the needy. Like Jesus, it says that Job was a *deliverer*. He delivered *the poor that cried*. He delivered *the fatherless*. He delivered *the helpless*.

Note: The Bible doesn't say that Job *felt* for the poor that cried or that he *prayed* for the fatherless or even that he *sympathized* with the helpless; it says that he *delivered* them! Like Jesus, Job didn't just leave hugs of compassion behind him. He left a trail of freedom in his wake.

Like Jesus with the thief on the cross, Job says that "the blessing of him that was ready to perish came upon me." Why? Because he "searched out" the cause that he "knew not." Job didn't hide out behind the gates of suburbia with his blindfold on and his personal space staunchly defended against all comers. When he heard about a need or an injustice, such as child prostitution, he got out of his comfort zone and went and *searched it out*. And, of course, true to form, Job didn't just do a brief Google search and then retire to bed a little better informed about the sad, sorry state of the world. No, when Job *searched out* a situation, he had very practical purposes in mind. Remember, he was a *deliverer,* and when his search led him to vile men prostituting innocent little girls we read that he "brake the jaws of the wicked, and plucked the spoil out of his teeth." This isn't a guy who sits around trying to "cast the vision." This is a guy who gets down in the trenches and gets the job done!

Job 29 says that righteousness covered Job like clothing covers a body. But why? What made him so righteous? Maybe it had something to do with the fact that he caused the widow's heart to sing for joy. Or that, like Jesus, he was eyes to the blind, and feet to the lame; or even more so because he was a father to the poor. In other words Job had the respect of God as a perfect and upright man because he was living out, on a daily basis, what James called pure and undefiled religion, which was to care for the widows and the orphans. If a pure and undefiled religion truly governed our lives—how we spent our time, how we spent our money—and every aspect of our existence, then it's not too hard to see how we just might end up being singled out by Jehovah as a perfect and an upright demonstration of His kingdom pattern.

But it wasn't only God who respected Job. Scripture says that because Job "delivered the poor that cried, and the fatherless, and him that had none to help him," and because Job "caused the widow's heart to sing for joy" and was "eyes to the blind, and feet...to the lame," and because Job was "a father to the poor: and the cause which I knew not I searched out," and because Job "brake the jaws of the wicked, and plucked the spoil out of his teeth"—because of this life of pure and undefiled religion—when "the young men saw [Job], they hid themselves: and the aged arose, and stood up. The princes refrained from talking, and laid their hand on their mouth. The nobles held their peace, and their tongue cleaved to the roof of their mouth."

Now that's respect. And not just from God, but from men. From young and old, from rich and poor, from commoner to king. Why? Because Job lived a life that they all knew they should be living but didn't have the guts to. Because Job had enough of the manly stuff to give his strength and wealth away to those who were weak and had nothing. Which, of course, is something that everyone admires, but which few are actually willing to do.

Job 29 is the poetry of the Bravehearted Gospel. This poetry is missing in our world today, and is in desperate need of being reinfused back into the body of Christ, where it belongs. We are missing that spiritual growl that delivers the poor that cry, causes the widow's heart to sing for joy, and breaks the jaws of the wicked. We are lacking the authority that causes the youthful petulance and brazenness to hide itself and the aged wisdom to arise and lend its ear. We have not been eyes to the blind, nor feet to the lame, nor fathers to the poor. There are causes all over this world that "we know not" and that we are not searching out. But this world, its orphans, its widows, its lame, and its destitute are waiting in the darkness for the Light of Life, whom only the church can bring.

What are we going to do about it?

We have lost the whiskery bassier tones of truth. We have become an unbalanced body strong on the charm but light on the real-life substance that gets the job done.

We need the grit of Job.

We need men and women filled with the stuff of this extraordinary twenty-ninth chapter.

And when that happens—when the bloodline of Job walks the earth again—watch out!

But the question that has been scratching around at the back of my mind for quite some time is this: How in the world did we ever end up abandoning something so grand, so powerful, and epic as the Bravehearted Gospel for such a weak and puny version of Christianity in the first place? And that is exactly the question this book is going to attempt to answer.

Three

SCRATCHING THAT ITCH

L et me give you some background.

I have come to the conclusion in life that I am unmistakably a man. And it's not just the biological stuff that gave it away; its a thousand little things that all scream to my consciousness that I'm of the manly persuasion. For instance, I enjoy sweating, love to fix things, and would eat Hormel chili out of the can if Leslie didn't force me to dump it onto a plate.

However, even though I am a whiskery, bassy-voiced man, I have a serious soft side. This soft side has garnered me some dirty looks over the years from those of the male gender who think it anti-male to listen to '80s love songs and get teary-eyed while watching *The Little Mermaid*. Add to my schmaltzy sensitivities the fact that I have written ten books that went out of their way to champion femininity, and you can understand why I have been labeled a "girl's man" by some of my detractors. And yes, there have even been those who have accused me of being prejudiced in favor of women over men. I'd like to say it's an absurd notion, but it's not altogether false.

You see, unlike many of my fellow males, I have a vision for the feminine expression of Christ to be beautiful, elegant, mighty, and strong once again in our culture. I truly yearn to see a kind of girl re-emerge in our modern world that possesses both the dignified beauty and grace of an Audrey Hepburn along with the strength and the radical, poured-out passion for Christ of an Amy Carmichael. I strongly believe that this striking combination of elegance and spiritual energy, beauty, and spiritual abandonment is what God intends to plant within the heart of a Christian woman.

But whereas such a topic would make for an engaging and much-needed book, *The Bravehearted Gospel* is not that book.

I have spent 13 years and ten books allowing my soft side to speak on behalf of femininity. But there is a manly side of me as an author that has been itching to find its voice for some time. I may be a champion of femininity, but I'm also a huge fan of masculinity. And to emphasize one to the exclusion of the other, historically, has never proven beneficial. So at risk of losing my lifetime membership to the "You go, girl, society," I'm going to do something quite daring within this book. For years, every male in my generation has been encouraged to get in touch with his *feminine side,* but I would like to propose in this book that the body of Christ needs to get in touch with its *masculine side.*

Gulp! Did I actually just write those words?

Before we go any further, and before you start associating the name Eric Ludy with rancid cabbage and curdled milk, I'd like to stop right here and clarify some of the terms I will use throughout the rest of this book.

For instance, what exactly do I mean when I say the body of Christ needs to get in touch with its *masculine side?*

Well, this isn't a concept that I just pulled out of thin air. As I said above, all my life I've heard over and over again from popular books, television, and culture that we men *need* to get in touch with our feminine side. Now, I didn't come up with this idea of a feminine side, but it seems to be something that everyone readily acknowledges both the existence and the definition of. This feminine side, from all that I've heard and been taught, is mostly a description of a handful of traits that everyone seems to agree are found more predominantly in women than in men, even though they are by no means exclusive to women. This includes things like tenderness, the ability to empathize and lend a listening ear, as well as an emphasis on the importance of open communication and the expression of feelings in relationships, to name a few. Everyone also seems to agree, including myself, that men, in general, would greatly benefit if they "got in touch" with a few pages of this feminine playbook and became a little more tender, relational, communicative, and understanding. What's to argue with here?

But a few years back, this thought began to dawn on me: If there's a feminine side to things, then there must also be a masculine side. And if getting in touch with our feminine side is a good thing to do wherever the feminine side is lacking, then it follows that getting in touch with our masculine side would also be just as beneficial wherever the masculine side of things is missing.

That way we have balance.

But I want to ask you a question: When was the last time you heard anyone in a popular book, on television, or culture suggest that *anyone*—man, woman, or child—would benefit from getting in touch with their masculine side?

Yep! I'm drawing the same blank.

Feminine expression and the feminine side are popular in our society, but masculine expression is not.

Political correctness aside, there *is* a list of traits in our culture that are classed as noble and good as well as feminine, and men and society are routinely encouraged to get in touch with them.

But where, I ask, is that list of traits classed as noble and good as well as masculine that women and society are routinely encouraged to get in touch with?

Are you drawing a blank again?

Well, that's why I'm writing this book.

This missing masculine side, or manly stuff as I often refer to it, is mostly a description of a handful of traits that *generally* are found more predominantly in men than in women, even though they are by no means exclusive to men—things like a willingness to wage war, a desire to fix what is broken, and a desire to conquer and to overcome, to name a few.

Now, some might ask, "Who are you, Eric, to be defining what's feminine and what's masculine?"

Well, first off, these feminine side and masculine side descriptions aren't *my* descriptions. Just pick up any relationship book, secular or otherwise, and you will find the above descriptions in just about every one that's been written within the past 30 years. They'll all tell you that men, in general, like to fix things and that women, for the most part, want to communicate their feelings, and so on, and so on.

But the problem comes when we begin to face the fact that the masculine side of things is just not politically, socially, or religiously correct anymore.

While most would agree, for example, that men are the ones who have traditionally waged war, it is rarely noted these days as to how this could possibly be anything but a flaw in the masculine constitution that needs to be done away with. "If women ruled the world," it is said, "there would be no war; for, unlike men, women would never send the children that they nursed to life to go off and die in some lonely, muddy ditch for nothing but power and worthless pieces of land."

This common feminine side versus masculine side description—that men are the warmongers while women are basically peacemakers—once again is not my own invention. It is quite simply popular opinion. Just google this if you don't believe me. This common point of view certainly acknowledges the existence of the warlike masculine side, but who in their right mind would encourage *anyone* to get in touch with it?

This perspective only sees monsters like Hitler rising from the "willingness to wage war" and *seems* to be more predominant in men than in women. But it sees nothing of the countless men who, propelled by that same willingness, died by the thousands across the killing fields of Europe to see Hitler stopped and his plans for world domination destroyed.

And yet it is precisely because of men like these, *and* their willingness to wage war, to give their lives, and spill their blood, that our children live out their days in the bright light of liberty instead of the shadow of the Swastika.

In light of the monumental problems that we are facing in the world and the church today, I for one believe that men, women, and society in general would greatly benefit if we got in touch with a few pages of the masculine playbook and started to once again become a little more willing to stand for what is right, wage war against what is wrong, fix what is broken, and press on until we conquer those things that are seeking to destroy us.

I realize this argument pokes at certain social sensibilities that are wired into our cerebral hard drives. But really, when you think about it, what's to argue with here?

After all, it only seems fair to me that if we are going to acknowledge the existence of a feminine side and encourage those who are missing it to get in touch with it, then we also need to acknowledge the existence of a masculine side and encourage those who are missing it to get in touch with it as well.

After all, it *is* God who created both male and female; and the unique abilities and emphases that He designed into the makeup of each sex are there for a reason. Far from being flaws, I'm convinced these differences have divine purposes and functions.

I honestly don't believe that the phrase "get in touch with your feminine side" is intended as a claim that all women are tender and understanding, or that all men are hard-hearted. It is, quite simply, a statement that *women,* whether men will admit it or not, have quite a few things that they tend to gravitate toward and seem to specialize in, and that from these things they have much to *offer* and we have much to *learn.*

Likewise, the phrase "we need to get in touch with our masculine side" is not claiming that all men are battle-hardened veterans for truth or that all women are weak and unwilling to fight. It is, quite simply, a statement that *men,* whether anyone will admit it or not, not only have something to *learn* from the feminine side but also have something to *offer.* It is a straightforward acknowledgment that there are things that *men* tend to gravitate toward and seem to specialize in, and that from these things they have much to contribute and we have much to gain.

In my bumbling way I am attempting to make a point on this rather awkward and incorrect topic. You see, as strange as this might sound to the human ear, the feminine side isn't *just* for women. Rather, it's for men, it's for children, as well as for women. It's for society, for doctrine, for the church, and for balance. But in choosing to term it the feminine side, it is just an easy way to refer to those parts of truth that most women seem to naturally express and excel in.

On this point few of us will probably disagree. It's when I mention that the body of Christ needs to get in touch with its "masculine side" that we all start shifting in our seats. After all, what does this Eric Ludy guy mean by *masculine side?*

Well, don't worry—the manly stuff referred to in this book is not going to be the "manly stuff" of Homer Simpson, Howard Stern, or Jimmy Kimmel. It isn't some backward, ignorant, brawling, pigheaded, perverted, obnoxious rendition of thinking and reasoning, living, and breathing.

In fact, quite to the contrary.

When talking about the manly stuff, I'm not talking about some category of truth that is distinctly or exclusively male, but rather that side of truth that men, by their very nature, are most attracted to and are most likely to express.

But here is the point I want you to catch: This masculine side isn't only for men. It's for children, it's for women, as well as for men. It is for society, for doctrine, for the church, and for balance.

This is a book about the restoration of balance.

It's a book about the manly stuff that's gone missing without ever being missed.

This is not a book from the *men* who "have it" to the *women* who "don't." But it is a heartfelt call to search out and find that God-given part of us that has gone missing from both our men *and* our women, from our children and our homes, from our church, from our society, and from our doctrine.

We need both the feminine side and the masculine side. An over-emphasis on either one to the exclusion of the other is nothing but error parading as truth.

And error kills.

Four

WHY CAN'T YOU BE MORE LIKE YOUR SISTER?

I remember being four-foot-five in the fourth grade. It bothered me that there were girls taller than me.

"Well, Eric," my mother consoled, "girls just mature faster than boys."

It's just a matter of scientific fact that boys take a while to warm up the maturation engine. But, whereas girls might be more attractive at every juncture of growth and development in the human life cycle, a fully matured, finely crafted, full-grown man is something to behold. And he is not at all like a girl—he is something majestically, intrepidly, daringly, durably, and totally "other." *He is a man.*

So, little girls mature faster and look prettier than little boys. It's simply a biological fact, and I am willing to admit it. And, in the same way, the fragrant, feminine truths within the Bible also generally mature faster within the soul and the church than do the more manly truths.

But in a healthy church there isn't supposed to be a choice between the feminine or the masculine side of truth, but a presentation of both in perfect harmony with the other.

Today, the manly stuff is missing. This manly stuff is deemed incorrect, unloving, and narrow-minded by our oversensitive culture, and the church is unwittingly playing right along. But when you remove the manly stuff from the body of Christ, you remove the horsepower from the engine of the church. When the manly stuff is absent—when men are not allowed to contribute what God gave them to contribute—then truth becomes more vulnerable to error, doctrinal problems remain unabated and unfixed, and biblical ideas are emptied of their muscle to perform. An emasculated church might smell sweeter and look nicer, and may even get in a whole lot less trouble, but ultimately, it is a church that is impotent. And while it might be less offensive, it is powerless to break through to the souls of the lost or to radically rescue the overlooked and the oppressed.

I grew up in a very healthy Christian home. I was loved dearly, corrected with grace, and daily encouraged in my uniqueness. Whereas the idea of strong masculinity wasn't vigorously promoted during my upbringing, it was also not diminished or hindered in any way. I guess you could call it a male-friendly-yet-male-neutral environment. However, I had (and still do have) an older sister who made my youthful boyishness appear rather tacky, unrefined, and petulant in contrast. My mother intensely loved me, but, no matter how hard she tried, she just couldn't restrain herself from saying the fateful words:

"Eric, why can't you be more like Krissy?"

And to be honest, I don't blame her. Krissy was sweet, and I was... well, I was something else. Krissy was clean, and I was covered in dirt and sweat. Krissy was quiet, and I was loud. Krissy was interested in spiritual things, and I was interested in football. Krissy was compliant, and I was strong-willed. Krissy was compassionate, and I was blunt. Krissy was perfumed, and I smelled like the local creek bed.

If this world were full of Krissys, it is hard not to imagine it being a far better place. Krissy is the most pleasant, courteous, loving, tenderhearted person whom I know. I often refer to her as the Mother Teresa of Michigan. My sister loves everyone and is loved by everyone. So, for my mother to wish her two youngest children (both boys) to be a bit more Krissy-ish in their nature definitely makes sense. However, the Ludy family would not be the Ludy family if it were just a gaggle of pleasant, courteous, loving, tenderhearted girls. For the Ludy family to become the dynamic life-giving organism that it now is, it needed the injection of two dirty, sweaty, loud, strong-willed, blunt, and smelly boys named Eric and Mark Ludy.

Why is it that every picture we see of Jesus seems to look kind of like Krissy—sweet, clean, quiet, compliant, compassionate, sweetly perfumed, and graced with an alabaster brow? I love everything about Krissy and I wouldn't change her in even the smallest way. But we need more than Krissys to make this Christian thing work in this world.

We've become so used to seeing Jesus portrayed holding pudgy babies and soothing lost little lambs that the idea of Him strolling into the temple armed with a whip to purge it of all its fleshly error seems jarringly foreign. Or, how about when Jesus stood toe to toe with the Pharisees and called them hypocrites seven times in one chapter,[1] as well as blind,[2] damned,[3] murdering serpents[4] who were the "unrighteous children of hell"?[5] This seems shocking language for gentle Jesus meek and mild. In fact, it even seems "un-Christian," doesn't it? How is that even possible? What has happened to our sensibilities when even Christ's own actions seem "un-Christlike" to our modern "Christian" mind? The only possible explanation is that we seem to be viewing Jesus not as He was, but through some sort of one-dimensional filter—a filter that strains every last ounce of masculinity, grit, or aggression out of the historical man Jesus Christ, a filter that is distinctly and overtly biased toward feminine sensibilities. It's as if the manly stuff has been surgically removed from the whole Christian mechanism and even from the way we think. It's almost as if, and I hate to use this word again, but it's almost as if we as the body of Christ have been unwittingly castrated. (That is my final use of that awful word—I promise.)

Five

BLOOD, DIRT, BUGS, AND MESS

When I was seven, I was licensed to kill. I must have shot down, beheaded, or otherwise chopped into little pieces over a thousand bad guys between my seventh and eighth birthday parties. But I can assure you it was all done for the cause of justice and for the preservation of liberty. I risked life and limb daily to make this world a better place, but I received not a single statement of thanks from anyone for all my heroism. In fact, all I ever really got was a dirty look from Mr. Walthers next door when he saw me using his flower garden as my personal Omaha Beach training ground.

If it wasn't bloodshed, it was dirt. At the age of seven, dirt was sexy. It doesn't make complete sense now, but I loved dirt, especially digging holes. My brother Mark and I once drew out the blueprint for an entire underground house that we were going to build. It didn't quite work out, but the idea transfixed me for months and I wore blisters into every part of my body attempting to make that dream a reality.

I wasn't as much of a bug-collecting boy, but my buddies sure did enjoy it. Steve, the kid from down on Oak Street, collected worms, grasshoppers, and roly-pollies. He had an ant farm on his bookshelf, a one-winged butterfly jammed into an empty peanut butter jar sitting on top of his nightstand, and the most disgusting assortment of crawdads living in a rather putrid and unsanitary fishbowl stationed on top of his messy dresser.

Blood, dirt, bugs, and mess—it's all part of boyhood. If it seems gross to an adult, it was probably at one time fun as a little boy. It's the snippish, snailish, and puppy dog tailish dimensions of life that make up the food of a young boy's existence. As the saying goes, if a boy isn't covered in dirt, with a scrape on his knee, a rock in his pocket, and doggy doo-doo on his shoe, then he's not really alive.

If we were to be honest, little boys are about as politically incorrect as they come. They are dirty, smelly, bug-collecting, sweat-drenched, killing machines that speak their minds far too freely. We put up with their "loathsome manner" nowadays mainly because we don't have much of a choice. But, as a culture, we have resolved that if we must endure their "incorrectness" now, we will make sure to squeeze every last drop of it out of them by the time they reach manhood, lest their poor wives, children, and the civilized world in general be forced to endure such reprehensible behavior for the entirety of these men's small-minded, left-brained lives.

I would like to draw a parallel here between little boys and certain truths within the Bible. There are ideas within the Bible, that, well, let's just say are bloody, dirty, and buggy. We all know these awkward snips, snails, and puppy dog tails are there, but we labor to cover them over with a blob of gel, a quick washcloth to the face, and a spritz of lemon water.

If you look closely, there are a lot of these little boy truths in the Bible. And we typically labor to explain them all away. But on the flip side, there are a lot of pleasant sugar-and-spice ideas in the Bible too—you know, the little girl truths. These we plaster on greeting cards, plaques, artwork, and necklaces. Could you imagine a greeting card that reads, "Why hath Satan filled thine heart to lie to the Holy Ghost?"[1] Whereas the statement might be straight out of Scripture, it's more a "little boy notion," and not very appropriate for a get-well card.

Now, I'm not one to send holiday cards that say things like, "All that will live godly in Christ Jesus shall suffer persecution. Merry Christmas, the Ludys."[2] I am a friendly sort of guy. If I were a dog I would probably be a serious tail waggin' licking machine. I love people and I love to see people feel important, valued, and happy. So as a Christian communicator, it seems rather obvious that if I'm going to speak on truth, I might as well emphasize all the sugar and all the spice that makes everyone feel all nice.

But pleasant little girl truths are like a handful of flowers. They are beautiful and smell wonderful, but if they are removed from the dirt (the little boy truths), and no longer take their root and find their nourishment in the grit of heaven, then their life quickly fades.

I'm tired of a version of Christianity that withers up in the hot sun. I'm tired of seeing happy believers grow stale and lose their impetus. I, for one, really like the beauty of the sugar and spice and would love to keep their fragrance around. But for these truths to thrive and blossom, we need to transplant all this girly stuff back into the dirt.

I've been a softie Christian for a long, long time. I would prefer not to refer to myself as a girly Christian, but for better or for worse, that is precisely what I have been. And once you get acclimated to applause, pats on the back, shouts of "Preach it, brother!" and hearty amens, when you speak, it's sort of difficult to let it all go. The sugar and spice *is* really, *really* nice. But I had a conversation with God a few years back that is messing with my softie state.

"God," I said, "I want the full package! I want to represent everything that You are. I want the version of truth that works, not the one that just looks good on the outside!"

There seems to be two sides to every truth: a soft side and a hard side, a hug side and a hammer side, a girly side and a manly side. And just like it takes both a man and woman's input and involvement to get pregnant and bear a child, it takes both of these sides of truth working in harmony to create true spiritual life.

The sugar and spice emphases of truth are much more pleasant, and this is why they lead the way in both society and the modern church. Again, girls mature faster than boys, and therefore begin to show the virtue of their sex sooner. The feminine side of truth is much more attractive and inviting and therefore much easier to proclaim.

Well, since curious minds want to know, here's how I would classify the feminine side of truth. It is...

- an emphasis on mercy and forgiveness
- an emphasis on beauty and allure
- an emphasis on relationship and unity
- an emphasis on acceptance and embracing
- an emphasis on feeling and intuition

These are critical components of a healthy church. If you are missing the feminine side of truth, I think it goes without saying that you are involved in a religious experience seriously lacking in the pleasant sugar-and-spice dimension of the gospel life.

Now let's take a look at the blood, dirt, bugs, and mess that the manly side of truth is responsible to bring to the table. I would classify the masculine side of truth as...

- an emphasis on holiness and righteousness
- an emphasis on conquering and achieving practical real-world goals
- an emphasis on repairing what is broken
- an emphasis on the accuracy of truth and the preservation of sound doctrine
- an emphasis on the just need to wage war for the right and to uproot the wrong

Not many of us nowadays are very attracted to that second list. No offense to the masculine side of truth, but please, mister, could you take a shower and get a shave and put on a little cologne? You reek with political incorrectness, legalism, and puritanical holier-than-thou bigotry. Let's be honest: If I give people the opportunity to pick from the above-mentioned two lists, who in the world is crazy enough to want list two?

You see, this is precisely why this book is going to be a bit uncomfortable. Because for us to truly understand the Bravehearted Gospel, we need to once again infuse some serious "hard hammer" into our Christian experience. To place no value or worth on what half of our race has been uniquely gifted by God to contribute is both a travesty and a loss—not just for men, but for all of society and the church. We need grit mixed back into the gospel. And if we are truly wanting the strength and potency of the gospel reborn in our lives and our generation, then we need to regain the manly stuff.

Now, I realize I've said this more than a couple times already, but I feel it's necessary to do it once more for all those inclined to throw this book out under the banner of a "chauvinistic rant." Just because I'm referring to the things in list two as the manly stuff doesn't mean that they are intended *just* for men. If men can get in touch with their feminine side, then women can get in touch with their masculine side.

Down through the ages, the church has been filled with women who had bravehearted grit at the bedrock of their existence. Vibia Perpetua, Elizabeth Fry, Amy Carmichael, Sarah Edwards, Esther Ahn Kim, Elisabeth Elliot, Sabina Wurmbrand, Catherine Booth, and Gladys Aylward are all heroes of the faith who bore the bravehearted crest on their spiritual armor. And there are thousands more. In fact, I could fill the rest of this book with stories of women who exemplified a balanced Christian life that showcased both of the lists above and more.[3]

I'll say it again: *The Bravehearted Gospel* is not a man's book, a man's truth, or a man's rendition of the Christian life. The Bravehearted Gospel is merely a return to the old-fashioned power of the Christian faith in which the feminine and the masculine reunite to bring a more complete picture of the kingdom of Jesus Christ to earth.

THE BRAVEHEARTED PATH

WHERE IT BEGINS

So who is Eric Ludy, and how did I end up writing this book on the Bravehearted Gospel?

I'm afraid that if you saw me on the streets, you wouldn't think that I'm a writer. Writers have an intellectual look about them, eyes filled with wisdom, and a bit more gray in their hair. I probably look more like a 19-year-old golf caddie home from college for the summer, still trying to figure out which end is up in life. I think my problem is that I have this boyish face and a serious absence of facial hair (there are 13-year-olds with thicker beards).

According to my birth certificate I'm 36, but try and convince the little girl at the park of that who, just yesterday, wanted to know if I was a kid or a grown-up. "I'm a grown-up," I said, not particularly fond of the sound of such a declaration. She just stared at me, trying to see how that was possible.

So, whether I look it or not, I am one of those 30-something Christians. And as a 30-something Christian, there is a certain mold that I should fit. Without a doubt I should be postmodern in my thinking. I should be more on the progressive, push-the-envelope side of theology and practice. And, after years of disillusionment and witnessing moral failure among the clergy of today, I should be continually on the verge of throwing it all away or at least just a little push from blowing a fuse and shaking my fist heavenward, crying, "Why, God? Why are You so impotent?!"

I must admit, I've toyed with postmodern mentalities, and I've considered pushing the envelope in my theology and practice in hopes that it might draw more people to Jesus Christ. And yes, I have faced some serious disillusionment in witnessing up close the moral fragility of our modern clergy.

Seven years ago I came to a breaking point. I loved Jesus, but detested this whole Christian system that bore His name. I wavered for quite a few months, walking that tightrope between cynicism and faith. But I found something in that journey that has made me even stronger through it all. When I came to the crossroads, and the choice between doubt or belief stood stark before me, I chose to shove all my chips into the center of the table and say, "I'm all in on Jesus." In my darkest night of the soul, I leaned harder than ever on my Savior and He proved Himself to me.

This is where the bravehearted path always begins.

It begins with brokenness, with desperation, with need, and with hunger.

Where does it end? No one knows. Its limits have never been tested, its depths never plumbed, and its boundaries never reached.

But it always *begins* in the same place.

The bravehearted path picks up at exactly that same point where all of the best laid plans of flesh and self crash and burn.

The bravehearted path is that vision that arises from the ashes of dreams, it is that life that erupts from the silent tomb of unbelief; it is that faith that rises to walk on the watery grave of doubt; and it is that beginning that begins only after everything else has come to an often bitter end.

The road that we walk is long; and when the going gets tough we can either give up, press on, or find a better way.

The bravehearted path is the end of our plans and the beginning of God's.

The bravehearted path *is* that more excellent way.

I believe that Christianity is at a very important crossroads. And it's not just Eric Ludy who needs to make a choice regarding which direction he is going to turn. Will we stay where we are, do what we've done, and continue to repeat the mistakes of our past? Will we emerge, press forward, and invade the future rejecting the comforting yet lethal embrace of the familiar? And if we do emerge, will we emerge in rebellion, recklessly abandoning the historic moors of our faith in our obstinate determination to drain freedom's cup to its last? Or will we emerge from stagnant religious routine to embrace, in living color and vibrant love, the Holy God of Scripture, and His ancient, eternal truth? I believe each of us needs to decide. Do we truly believe that God is alive and that His Word is authoritative, or will we allow the culture and the times to dictate the version of Christianity that we espouse? Will we shove all our chips into the center and say, "I'm all in on Jesus"? Or will we let doubt slowly continue to erode and poison our faith? It's that simple.

I am a man who historically has loved to be liked, and I have oft clipped the wings of my message to make it as appealing as possible to the largest conceivable crowd. I have told my audience to receive when they needed to be told to repent, and I have "taught" the truth of Christ when my audience needed to me to "preach" the Word of God with thunder. I have lacked the manly stuff for most of my ministry career. I have, in many ways, been cowardly when God needed a man who was courageous.

I have grown up in the corridors of the church, and am all too familiar with its inadequacies and, like many others, sometimes struggle with recognizing its strengths. I am not one inclined to compliment the modern church, but I must say that with a degree of passion that never ceases to perplex me, I love Christ's body and yearn to see it know Him, be perfected, and find the fullness of His love and His life. As the apostle Paul said, "I am compelled to preach the gospel."

Eric Ludy is a guy who rarely offends. You see, for most of my life I have avoided purposely making my audience squirm with discomfort, for it violates a part of who I am. It is that tolerant part of me that is always yearning to make everyone happy, be liked, and say the thing that will make me popular with the majority of those present. The first time my fingers touched the keypad of my laptop to begin work on this manuscript my heart was thumping and I could feel the beads of sweat beginning to bubble up along my temples. This work, in many ways, is the opposite of Eric Ludy, but in many ways it is the opus of my life.

I realize this book is unusual. But that is simply due to the fact that it is seeking to do something that feels foreign today within the corridors of the church. But I hope and pray that this book's uniqueness proves its value and not its abandonment. Whether this book sells or not, Leslie and I are headed full steam in this direction. We have tasted the brave-hearted life and, let me tell you, it is very good!

I have spent more time praying in the past ten months of my life than all my life leading up to it multiplied by seventeen. This has been a season set apart for Jesus unlike any period of my life before. Leslie and I have spent hours each day pleading with God for more and more of His grace, pleading that somehow Christianity today would encounter the grandeur and majesty of our King and Lord. We long for the God of the Bible to be the God of the Christian faith once again.

These ten months have left us empty of self and ready to be filled. The grand blueprint that I had drafted for my life has been burned, and in its place the bravehearted path now stands. Leslie and I have been broken by the Spirit of God at a deeper level than I can ever remember being broken, and we have been inspected by His bright light of truth down to the marrow of our bones. He has stood our lives up against His perfect Word and then gently asked us to "Behold the disparity." We are leaders in this whole "Christian thing" and God has tenderly revealed the painful reality to our souls that our lives have been, even in minis-try, false and conceited in many different ways. If manly stuff is missing in the body of Christ, then the blame includes us.

I've noticed that throughout history, when the fire of revival over-takes a community, everything in that community shuts down. The theaters close, the bars shut down their operations, and every store along Main Street hangs a sign on the door that reads, "Closed until further notice." For us, this has been a season of soul revival. Every-thing of entertainment has somehow disappeared from our lives. No movies, no television, no novels, no gaming, no radio, and no newspa-per. Everything that could possibly distract us from God's presence has just vanished from our existence. We haven't purposely avoided these things; they have simply disappeared out of our lives. Our lives have been shut down to the flesh and opened up wide to the Spirit. And, as dull and as boring as that may sound, we have been tasting heaven on earth. We have unearthed a kind of soul entertainment that is breath-takingly majestic and profound. Our hearts are ravished by the beauty of our King Jesus, and there is a desperation in our souls to help others find what we are tasting. We feel the necessity to share this fire and pass on this revival.

It is out of this soul desperation that I am writing this book. I am being nudged by God to speak boldly in these upcoming chapters. And that is something that is tremendously uncomfortable for me to do. I've historically been a people-pleaser and an ovation-gatherer. But God is branding the bravehearted crest onto my forehead, saying, "In all you do, Eric, in all you say, you represent Me! May they see it and know what it means!"

An untold number of Christian men over the past 18 years of my life have said to me, "When I was your age, Eric, I was just like you." What these well-meaning pastors and leaders were attempting to say—indirectly—is, "I too was once all spit and snarl for the gospel, but, Eric, calcification eventually reaches every Christian leader's soul—it's just a matter of time!"

Please, dear God, don't let me become as these men! Don't let me stop short! Don't let me pitch my tent in this land of mediocrity! Don't let me accept defeat and subjection as my lot in life! But rather, make me fit to go the distance as a fighter, a wrestler, an athlete, a soldier, a man. And please don't let this book be shallow religious tripe, but please help this to be real, help me to be vulnerable, and help me to effectively and courageously pass on this amazing life, love, and grace that You have entrusted to me. I know I'm unfit to have my name on the front of this book, but may it be a lifelong reminder to me of the high call You have upon my life and my generation.

My intent in this book is not to make enemies. As I said, I'm a guy who likes to be liked. But I'm willing to lay that down, if necessary, to speak this message. I tremble even as I say that. I am merely pleading for truth, unaltered by the passing of time, to once again reign in the corridors of the church. I am begging for an honest analysis of our current state as a Christian system, and it is my hope that this book can inspire a new manner of living, a new manner of conversation, and a new manner of growth as a result.

The bravehearted path is real to me—powerfully real! I've seen it proven at the tire-tread level of my life day in and day out for years. And I'll go beyond putting my name on the cover of this book; I am also willing to give up my life for the atomic truth stowed away inside these upcoming pages.

If I unintentionally ruffle your feathers somewhere in this book, and an urge to stick my head in a toilet and flush begins to overcome you, then if it helps, please grab yourself a plunger, stick it in the nearest toilet and flush. I even give you the license to imagine it is me the whole time because I'm sure I deserve it for something, even if it isn't for what is in this book.

Let me finish this chapter with a quote from A.W. Tozer:

> The true church has never sounded out public expectations before launching her campaigns. Her leaders heard from God and went ahead wholly independent of popular support or the lack of it—sometimes to triumph, oftener to insults and public persecution—and their sufficient reward was the satisfaction of being right in a wrong world. Yes, if evangelical Christianity is to stay alive she must have men again, the right kind of men. She must repudiate the weaklings who dare not speak out, and she must seek in prayer and much humility the coming again of men of the stuff of prophets and martyrs are made of.[1]

Tozer wrote those words 47 years ago. And if they were true words then, they are even more true now. The church desperately needs the stuff of the Bravehearted Gospel back in the very marrow of its bones if it even hopes to survive this generation.

Part Two

An Ode to Homer

A study in incorrectness and irrelevance

Six

OF DYING HORSES AND SHOTGUNS

I don't know if you are uncomfortable yet with reading this book. I can honestly say that I'm thoroughly uncomfortable with writing it.

It's funny, but though I am fully aware that this manly stuff needs to be reinfused back into the church, there is a very loud part of me right now that is wishing someone else had taken this job. But we all know whoever is stupid enough to write five chapters on such an "incorrect" topic is not smart enough to know when to stop. So I press onward.

Imagine a scene from an old black-and-white cowboy movie: a horse is mortally wounded; she rears back her head in pain as her mournful cry echoes out into the night. A man and a woman stand at the door of the stall, grimacing at the sight. They love this horse.

Imagine the woman, a beautiful young thing with a bow in her hair, rouge on her cheeks, and a shotgun in her hand, saying, "Carl, I think we are going to have to put the poor creature down." At hearing such a pronouncement, Carl, a burly man in a cowboy hat and leather boots, screams, "No, Jane! You're not going to shoot Trixie! You just can't!" Carl dramatically leaps in the direction of Trixie and throws his massive body on top of her, sobbing with great and unfettered emotion. Meanwhile, the beautiful young girl whispers, "Carl, it's best for Trixie. There is nothing more that can be done. If you really love her, you'll let her go."

Can anyone tell me what's wrong with this picture?

Well, first of all, it's never been put into a single film that's been released by Hollywood. Why? Because even Hollywood intrinsically knows that something isn't right about it. It just doesn't seem appropriate for Carl to be such a sap and it seems strange for Jane to be so unfeeling. But ironically, if the roles were reversed, for some reason, it's not at all uncomfortable for Jane to feel such strong compassion for Trixie, and it seems totally normal that Carl is less emotive and more willing to do what must be done.

In a general sense, there is a way that we know men should be and there is also a way that we know women should be. And whether it's politically correct to acknowledge or not, the truth is that we all instinctively know what falls under the banners of feminine and masculine behavior.

I realize that I might sound a bit overconfident in making such a claim, so let's press on and see if we can't come to a point of agreement on this matter.

My buddy Ben is the kind of guy who says it like it is. I am often laboring to add a little more polish to his plain and simple clarifications of reality, but all in all, the guy is just saying what everyone would agree with if we weren't so encrusted with all our cultural sensitivities. In fact, the idea of the "dying horse" has come up in conversation quite a few times between us. And I'll never forget the very first time that it did.

"A man would just kill the poor thing and put it out of its misery!" Those were Ben's precise words.

And I must admit I was rather offended. It wasn't that what he was saying was wrong. It's just that it seemed so heartless, uncaring, unfriendly, and hostile toward this wounded horse.

You see, I grew up in a culture where dying horses were to be cared for, lovingly held, and pampered with morphine until their last breath. This Ben guy was brutal. I secretly nursed the thought, *You horse killer, you!*

"I know what you're thinking," Ben said, reading my mind. "You're thinking that what I just said was heartless, uncaring, unfriendly, and hostile, aren't you?"

I shifted uncomfortably in my seat, which just happened to be a booth at Perkin's Family Restaurant.

"Well," I stammered, "it just seems that…"

"A man has to be willing to make the hard decision, Eric." Ben interjected. "It's not a decision that is heartless, uncaring, unfriendly, and hostile—it's actually the most loving, compassionate thing to do. But it takes serious guts to pull the trigger."

I instinctively stiffened. Ben's voice was far too loud. I didn't want anyone to hear this socially incorrect and outlandish discussion. After all, I was a respected member of this community. It was then that I started thinking to myself that we should have had breakfast in Ben's hometown instead of mine.

Truth is harmless as long as it stays locked inside the dormitory of the mind. The problem comes in when this truth escapes out of the polite lair of the cerebrum and grabs a hold of the tongue and starts talking, grabs a hold of the hands and starts wrestling, grabs a hold of the feet and starts walking.

But I, for one, am not interested in a harmless truth or a harmless God. Give me a truth that works, and a God who makes me tremble.

Seven

CARL VS. JANE—
A LOSING PROPOSITION

M en and women are different.

I guess the truth of that statement should be both obvious and self-evident. But it is amazing just how heightened and trained our social sensibilities have become. We all know that there are certain things that just are not supposed to be said. Even if they are true, you just don't speak them. And this whole masculine/feminine thing is definitely one of them.

Now, I'm not generally one to throw caution to the wind and to rush in where angels fear to tread, but I do feel that to get to the bottom of this issue we need to take just a minute to look a little closer at the two characters from earlier, Carl and Jane. But this time let's put them in their natural roles, with Carl playing the part of a figuratypic* man and Jane the part of a figuratypic woman.

Let's start by looking at Carl.

Carl, the manly man, sees that Trixie the horse is mortally wounded and should be put down.

And yet Carl's decision to put Trixie down isn't motivated by anger or testosterone or a desire to wage war. He wants what's best for Trixie. He loves Trixie, but after evaluating the facts it seems clear there's nothing that can be done except to put her out of her misery. It's not a fun decision to make. It's not macho, and it's not a power play. That, my

---

* *Figuratypic*—meaning pertaining to natural tendency (i.e., birds fly, houses are built of wood, and CDs carry music—whereas these often are true, they are not always true). Figuratypic is different than stereotypic, which is simply a blanket generalization based on prejudice and misinformation.

friends, is compassion guided by truth. And it's not something we see too often these days.

Yeah, Carl!

Now on the flip side, Jane, the girly girl, feels that Trixie should be kept alive as long as possible and kept far away from Carl's shotgun.

And yet Jane's decision to protect Trixie isn't motivated by ignorance or stupidity. She wants what's best for Trixie. She loves Trixie, yet she knows the facts, just like Carl does. She's not stupid, but she is hoping for a miracle. She wants to see Trixie whole again. That is no easy thing to believe for. And it's not weakness or frailty. The Bible says that love hopes and believes for all things. That, my friends, is compassion guided by love.

Yeah, Jane!

But here's where it gets weird. For some reason, Jane's expression of compassion is the only version seen as legitimate in the church and much of society today, even though it does not always lead to the correct course of action. Carl's instincts are deemed off-base, harsh, and unfeeling.

Now, a person looking to undermine what I'm saying could try and use what I just said as proof that Eric Ludy believes that truth is the exclusive domain of men while love is the sole domain of women. But that's *not* at all what I am saying.

Carl loves Trixie, yet his actions and compassion are guided *more* by facts and truth than the feelings he has for his horse. Jane knows the truth about Trixie, yet her actions and compassion are guided *more* by love and hope than by the facts she knows about Trixie's condition.

Both women and men have access to the same virtues of love, joy, peace, truth and valor, and so on. But certain of these qualities seem to find native soil in the heart of a woman and seem to grow more vigorously there, while others seem to take root and thrive more prominently in the hearts of men.

Men and women both have equal opportunity to grow in all the graces, and yet they seem naturally inclined to gravitate toward and excel in different ones.

When faced with a mortally wounded horse, men and women, Carl and Jane, who both have truth and love and are both wanting to act compassionately, will quite often come to very different conclusions as to what that compassion should look like.

This is not because of some deficiency of love in Carl or a lack of truth or understanding in Jane. It is due to a God-given, God-ordained difference in emphasis between the sexes. And ironically, it is God who planted these differences into the human race for us to enjoy, cultivate, and nurture.

Neither the male nor female propensities, leanings, preferences, or emphases were ever supposed to be crowned as the "correct" view. You know, as in the "correct" way to handle everything from relationships, to business, to church, to children, or for that matter, the problem of a dying horse. The feminine application of truth is not always the best course of action in all situations, such as Trixie's, and neither is the masculine emphasis always appropriate.

In all these things and a thousand more besides, neither the male nor female perspective was supposed to emerge victorious, but rather a blend of the two working side by side and arm in arm. Man and woman—male and female—were to become one flesh and learn from each other's strengths while acknowledging and abandoning their own weaknesses. And it is in this context, and only in this context, that we will fully see what God intended humanity to be.

Are you with me in realizing that something has clearly gone awry? We seem hyperallergic to the pollen of masculine behavior and thinking. And it isn't the first time in history that an imbalance of gender leanings overtook society.

For centuries the feminine emphasis was slighted, if not ignored altogether, as so inferior and deficient to the male emphasis as to have nothing of value to contribute to anything of importance.

Just take a quick peek at the dour and somber photos from the 1800s. You can almost hear the photographer in the background yelling out, "If anyone smiles I'll shoot you with my Colt .45!" There just wasn't a lot of sugar and spice flowing around back then. And when you remove the feminine emphasis it seems that everyone starts looking like they just got done drinking creek water out of their smelly boot before slicking back their hair with possum grease. No one in their right mind would wish for a return to those days, and yet in many ways we have come full circle, only this time on the opposite side of the coin.

It used to be that man was king—his views, his leanings, his tastes, and his impulses *alone* were what defined society. And society suffered greatly because of it. And whereas women were once falsely painted as the nonsensical and foolish sex, it is now the male—the blundering Homer Simpson—who wears the crown of the arch-idiot, as his wife, Marge, patiently doles out sage advice and waits indefinitely for her moronic husband to come to his senses.

Some would say that what goes around comes around and that men are finally getting what they deserve. And I fully agree—*we are!* But this justification is little more than sanitized revenge—an eye for an eye and a tooth for a tooth. And that's all well and good as long as you don't mind living in a sightless, toothless world.

I personally want to live in a world that works.

The things that God has uniquely crafted into the natures of men to contribute to their society, their marriages, their homes, and their churches are now treated like a preschooler's artistic scribblings. Whereas they might be pinned up on the fridge as cute, they are certainly not to be taken seriously as if they were the work of a bona fide artist.

Let's look at a few "for instances."

Men in our society are mocked as romantic nitwits. Let's admit it. For some reason it is socially acceptable for us all to chuckle at the complete and utter stupidity of men in the arena of love and relationships.

Why is it that men are, supposedly, so doltish in this all-important sphere of life? Rumor has it that we as men have been cursed with the most odious problem of being naturally prone to fix things instead of being inclined to listen. In other words, men try to fix a girl's problem instead of providing an understanding shoulder to cry on. In the relationship world, this is a big no-no. I personally have clarified this error to hundreds of thousands of young men over the past 13 years.

"If you want to win a girl's heart," I have counseled the male masses, "then become a student of her. When she is crying, don't try to fix her problem, but rather, put your arm around her and let her know you are there for her and wish to understand her pain."

This is classic relationship advice offered by yours truly. And to be honest, it works really well. As I said earlier, we men have much to learn from our mothers, sisters, and wives; and if we not only listen but act, we become better men for it.

Men are built to fix things, but in the process of training them in the art of love and romance, modern society has basically told them that their instinct to fix is incorrect and that to succeed in any form of relationship they must deny this instinct and learn to do something completely opposite their natural bent. It seems that we are being told that what we possess, as men, is trivial, our instincts are off-base, and what God gave us to contribute is of little to no value. And if we wish to save our marriages, then we first must deposit our gruff and unrefined nature in the nearest rubbish receptacle and then sit at our wife's feet to learn the "correct" way to conduct a relationship.

It seems, once again, that what a woman has to contribute is valid, but what a man brings to the table is not.

Now, whereas this "sensitivity thing" is a wonderful skill for men to learn in the art of relating to a woman, it is critically important that a man's desire to fix things not be surgically removed from his masculine tool chest. It's one thing to be understanding in a relationship, but if the problems inherent in a relationship are never *fixed* and made right, then these same conflicts and dilemmas will continue to resurface throughout a married life.

We need fixers. Think about it: We fully acknowledge the usefulness of a man who does not simply understand our plumbing problems but who fixes them. We supremely value the man (and most of them *are* men) who receives our broken-down vehicle not to merely cry with us over our misfortune but to miraculously return said vehicle to our possession in fully functioning and operable condition. We value fixers in every area of life. Men are natural fixers. Why, then, are men being told to check their emphasis at the door of their relationships as well as in so many other areas of their lives? It is sadly because we live in a society and attend churches that do not correctly appraise the value of the manly stuff.

If we have spent any time being intellectually honest about the way male-female relationships work, then we would have to acknowledge that we do categorize male and female behavior into clearly defined lists. And even though it is politically incorrect to say it, we all know it—men like to fix things, and girls like to be understood. And again, if we were to be honest, according to our society and the modern church, the girls have it right, while the men are the problem.

Score: Men 0, Women 1

Let's take another look at Carl and Jane through this twisted lens.

Carl wants to kill Trixie. Carl is insensitive and unresponsive to Jane's pleas for mercy and continues to narrow-mindedly push his bloody, testosterone-driven agenda that Trixie must die.

"*Men!*" Jane hisses in disgust through clenched teeth as she fervently begs for the life of her friend. With tears in her eyes, she searches Carl's hardened face for a trace of understanding or kindness but finds only mindless determination.

All right, all right, you get the idea.

When looked at through this lens, it is little more than an elaborate way of saying that Jane is good and Carl is evil. Basically, the feminine, nurturing emphasis is confirmed as "correct" while the masculine emphasis is dismissed as a relic of a bygone era. This is social prejudice at its worst, where men are condemned as unfeeling horse killers and women are seen as compassionate champions of life.

Score: Men 0, Women 2

So what does all this about wounded horses have to do with Christianity?

Well, let's see.

Eight

MEAN OL' PASTOR CARL

If you thought that chapter 7 was uncomfortable, wait until you get a load of this one. I'm about to introduce you to mean ol' Pastor Carl.

Let's first remove Carl's cowboy hat, boots, and shotgun and dress him up a little with a coat and tie. And let's stick him behind a mahogany desk inside some pastor's office in a small Midwestern town.

So Carl, in our story, instead of being a cowboy, is now a pastor, and let's make Jane a member of his church. Now, this next one might seem a bit odd, but let's say that instead of a wounded horse, Trixie is actually Jane's 20-something son, who also attends Carl's church.

Carl has himself a doozy of a problem.

You see, Jane's son is not doing so hot. In fact, he is living in blatant and unrepentant sexual sin. Carl has spent quite a large chunk of his time these past months tending to this rather messy mess. He has confronted the boy about the situation, he has pled with him to seek help and turn the spiritual corner on this nasty sin, but even after every attempt has been made to remedy the problem, the boy still persists in his lustful pursuit of pleasure. He just refuses to change his ways.

So what does Carl do? He doesn't seem to have a lot of options. Think about it: If he just turns a blind eye and shrugs his shoulders, it would be little more than silent endorsement to this boy's life of sexual indulgence. And what about all those young girls in the church whom this kid is making improper advances toward? If Carl does nothing, it is entirely possible that this kid may eventually end up stumbling them, dragging them down into his own sin.

If Carl allows this boy to continue his pretense of being a Christ-follower, what message does this send to the world about the nature of Christianity? What message does it send to the others within the church about the importance of sexual purity? And what message does it send to Jane's son about the perilous state of his own eternal soul?

You see, Carl has himself a doozy of problem.

Carl searches the Scriptures for guidance. He loves this young man. He wants what's best for him. But he finds that the Bible clearly states that when someone reaches this point, when someone has been confronted numerous times with his sin and yet still obstinately refuse to repent, then he is to be removed from the church fellowship lest he bring disgrace to the name of Jesus, lest the body of Christ become corrupted, and lest he gain false hope, from his now-empty religion, that all is well with his soul.[1]

Please note: I'm wriggling in my seat just writing this little ditty. Even my own sensibilities are so highly tuned to ferret out the manly stuff that it is hard for me, the writer of this book, to actually write what the manly stuff would do in such a situation.

With a heavy heart, Carl calls the young man to set up yet another appointment, but the kid refuses to even speak with Carl about the issue at hand. So Carl meets with Jane, the boy's mother, who upon hearing of Carl's proposed course of action, reacts in horror as if Carl were standing over the body of her wounded son with a shotgun.

"You can't do this to him, Carl, you just can't," she cries. "You'll kill him. He'll never come back to God if this is how he's treated. Aren't we as Christians supposed to be known by our love? Where's the love in this? I mean, I know he's messed up, but what he needs right now is love and understanding, not some ancient brand of holier-than-thou, condemning legalism! Why in the world would you want to kick a man when he's down?"

Carl hangs his head. He hates this. But someone has to do it.

"Jane, I understand how you feel, I really do. But your son has left me no choice. I'm sorry, but there's no other way."

"No other way?! What about the way of Jesus, Carl? It seems that I remember Jesus hanging out with sinners and drunks and prostitutes. So where do you get off with this idea that you're holier than Jesus was? Because, I can promise you one thing—Jesus sure wouldn't have had any problem being around my boy!"

"Jane, it's not—"

"No! No more. You've said enough. It's obvious that you are not the kind of pastor I thought you were. And if I had known better, I would have never brought my son here in the first place. The church is supposed to be a hospital! What kind of shepherd beats his sheep instead of tending to their wounds? What my son needs, Carl, is not some macho pep talk about right and wrong. What he needs is someone who will listen to him, someone who will put his arms around him and try to understand what he's going through. But all you want to do is treat him like he's a problem that needs to be fixed instead of a person. You sound just like my husband. All you're concerned about is making sure that he's not an embarrassment to you anymore. Well, I don't know what you call that, Carl, but I know one thing—it isn't love!"

Score: Men 0, Women 3

It isn't love. It isn't loving. It isn't Christian. It isn't Christlike.

Doesn't that sound familiar?

These are all terms that have been used over the years to describe why Christians shouldn't oppose homosexuality, why they shouldn't say divorce is wrong, and why they shouldn't cry foul over the killing of unborn children. Yes, I readily admit that these are touchy subjects and that they should be handled with gracious dexterity. But is it true that it isn't loving, Christian, or Christlike to speak and act forthrightly about these things?

We have so fully embraced the side of God's love that is most often and most naturally expressed by women that we have excluded the possibility of anything else. And if something or someone, such as Pastor Carl, dares to come along with a tune that doesn't quite keep step with this rhythm, it is dismissed with a wave of the hand and a flippant "That's not love," as if nothing more need be said on the subject.

But there *is* another side to God's love, and it is the side that is most often and most naturally expressed by men—if and when they are allowed to do so without being scorned as un-Christian and un-Christlike. In fact, it is this side of God, not only of His love but of His very nature, that this book is all about. And it's not only for men—it's also what women, children, and the church in general are missing. It is the manly stuff.

Pastor Carl is not the only man to run into this doozy of a problem. It just so happens that the apostle Paul stumbled across this precise mess in his day, too.

So what did Paul do?

Brace yourself for this one.

Turns out there was a guy in the church at Corinth who was sleeping with his father's wife. Which, by the way, isn't a good thing to do. The man was unrepentant and brazen in his sin. Paul did something so outrageously uncomfortable and socially incorrect that it's almost too difficult to mention. Paul rebuked unequivocally the overly tender and accommodating church at Corinth by saying, "I verily, as absent in body, but present in spirit, have judged already, as though I were present, concerning him that hath so done this deed. In the name of our Lord Jesus Christ, when ye are gathered together…deliver such a one unto Satan for the destruction of the flesh, *that the spirit may be saved* in the day of the Lord Jesus."[2]

Did Paul just say what I thought he said?

"In the name of our Lord Jesus Christ…deliver such a one unto Satan for the destruction of the flesh"? Now that doesn't sound very culturally sensitive or seeker-friendly. Was Paul crazy? What was he doing attaching the name of Jesus to such an unloving statement? Didn't he know that God is love?

Paul didn't say this because he hated the young man or because he didn't have the ability to put his arm around the young man's shoulder and listen. He said it because he loved him. And he loved the man enough to tell him the truth: that his unruly, indulgent flesh had to be destroyed so that his spirit could truly live. Whether we like it or not, Paul was simply saying, "It's time to shoot the horse."

Paul wanted this young man to face his sin without the false comfort of religion to ease his conscience. He wanted him to become desperate and disgusted with his lifestyle so that he would come back to Jesus not proud and defiant, but broken and contrite, so that his spirit would be saved on the day of judgment. For Paul knew that God gives grace only to the humble and that He resists the proud with an iron hand.

This is the manly stuff.

This is the manly side of love.

This is the manly side of truth.

And this is precisely what is missing from the heart and life of the church.

Contrary to how you might be perceiving me right about now, I've always been the "nice" guy. I'm not your typical "hard hammer" sort of fellow who always has a furrowed brow and something serious to say. Believe me, it was not my life's ambition to don a coat and tie and become like mean ol' Pastor Carl. I love to laugh. In fact, I *really* love to laugh. And I can testify that regaining the manly stuff has not in the least bit removed this side of my personality. If anything, it's enhanced it. I now laugh more than ever before.

You see, adding the manly stuff back into the body of Christ doesn't have to be a stroll down legalism lane, or for that matter, a dour judgment-fest on the church. But it also isn't all hugs and kisses. It's not scowls and disapproving grimaces, but it's not going to be giggles and snickers either. Putting the manly stuff back into the body of Christ is sort of like scaling Mount Everest—it's fun, but it's serious fun. It's difficult, but it's the adventure kind of difficult, not the sit-in-a-basement-closet-with-the-lights-off-and-see-how-long-you-can-handle-the-isolation kind of difficult.

So, welcome to Everest. Over the rest of this book we're going to work together to put the manly stuff back into the body of Christ, starting with ourselves. I promise it will be a supremely uncomfortable mission, outrageously awkward at times, even painfully difficult. But if you can hang with me until the end, I believe it may prove one of the most significant operations you might ever endure.

The
Bravehearted
Path

The Ground Rules

The idea of the bravehearted path is like a gentleman's war. It is made up of the stuff of battle, blood, guts, courage, frays, and guttural war cries, but it also has the dimension of dignity rolled into the whole affair. For instance, it is marked by valor, allegiance, honor, selfless sacrifice, love, and loyalty to the Commander, and the grace of noblesse oblige.

The bravehearted path is all about nobility and honor. In fact, it is the stuff of an entirely different time period. It's more Sir Walter Scott than John Grisham. It's more the timeless grandeur of Handel's *Messiah* than the hip artistry of Coldplay. It's the strength and dignity of knighthood woven into the fabric of our modern tapestry. You could almost say that it is kind of like transporting the spirit, grit, passion, and nobility of William Wallace back into our modern age and turning him loose on the streets of New York City. It's ancient truth invading the corridors of modern Christianity and turning it inside out.

I absolutely love the idea of the bravehearted path. It transforms Christianity from being a social club into a fellowship of the mighty. It turns mere males into men of fire, and mere females into women of valor. It's strength, dignity, passion, power, love, and truth all combined into one dynamic lifestyle and worldview. It's like a bolt of lightning to the soul. And, wow! Is it ever majestic!

The life, tradition, and power of the bravehearted path is governed by a sacred code of honor (which is a topic deserving of an entirely different book). It is governed by the life of God's Spirit, living, moving, and having His being at the very helm of the Christian soul. And it is governed by the single thought, "For the kingdom and for the glory of my King!" in every circumstance, of every minute, of every day.

Most of us are used to a rendition of truth that lacks manly stuff in its presentation. We are not familiar with the tone of the Bravehearted Gospel. So, I must prepare you by saying that when truth is once again spoken with masculine emphasis, it causes us to draw back at first.

- It's a stronger voice than we are used to hearing. It is by no means arrogant, but it feels much too confident for a society bred on the etiquette of relativism.

- It's a more courageous voice. It will risk the good opinion of an audience in order to secure the good opinion of God. And to a Christian culture crafted after the parameters of social correctness, such a voice feels foreign and even unfeeling.

- It's a more convicting voice. It dares to be specific and not general in its application of truth. It knows that people first often squirm before they are saved.

- It's a more passionate voice than is typically acceptable. It speaks truth with a volume and energy usually reserved for athletes and fans celebrating during a sporting event. And to a docile society familiar with the truth of Christ being served with tea and crumpets, this is akin to bringing the Texas A&M marching band to a Scrabble competition—it just feels like too much.

This short list is merely to prepare you. For it sounds all good and well to bring back the manly stuff to the body of Christ—that is, until you realize what that actually means.

If you were to see your right kidney sitting out on the kitchen counter and you thought, *That might be a good thing to put back in its rightful place,* you would find that there is a bit more to it than slapping the thing up against your body, hoping that it would stick. This will involve some serious spiritual surgery accompanied by a lot of practical stitching to hold the thing in place.

If you are the sort of person who likes a challenge, then you will relish the bravehearted path.

If you are the sort of person who feels fragile and constantly vulnerable, then you need the bravehearted path.

And if you are the sort of person who is scared of a soul confrontation, then I can think of no greater medicine for your fear than the brave-hearted path.

Oh, and if you are the sort of person who is predisposed to be against any and all things male, I hope and pray that the love, power, and passion enfolded in the bravehearted path will set you free from those tiresome shackles and allow you to see masculinity with new eyes and a new heart.

Let me quickly tell you about the writing of a Christian book:

When you write a Christian book nowadays, there are two basic guidelines that you must stick by. One, you must sound humble, open-minded, searching, and willing to enter a conversation. And, two, you must make your audience feel good about themselves. After all, what idiotic consumer would actually buy a book that makes them feel uncomfortable?

These two guidelines, for the most part, make total sense. If an author sounds pompous, closed-minded, unbending on his views, and unwilling to be questioned on his position, it doesn't breed much love, or much respect for that matter, between him and his audience. And if people all feel miserable by the time they finish reading a book, well, that doesn't seem very Christian now, does it?

But there is another factor that for some reason has been overlooked as of late in the Christian book-writing world.

When truth is spoken with the strength and tone of *the bravehearted*, there are times that it may not sound soft and gentle. Jesus employed a *bravehearted* voice and often times crowds walked away muttering to themselves about his gall. A *bravehearted* voice is forthright, bold, daring, and courageous. It is willing to speak the one thing that desperately needs to be spoken, which no one else is willing to say. A *bravehearted* voice is not devoid of love, it just employs love with both the "hug *and* the hammer" as it is defined in the Bible and not as it is defined in modern culture.

This book will unabashedly hold a bravehearted tone. It will be more confident than maybe you feel it should be and it will place an almost relentless pressure upon you as a reader to not just sit there, but do something. But I plead with you to give this book a shot. Try it. Experience the *bravehearted* voice. Allow it to make you uncomfortable. Allow it to acquaint you with a version of Christianity that actually triumphs with love and grace, flexing the muscles of God for this entire world to behold and take notice. I honestly believe you will love it, even though it might take you awhile to acclimate to the different tone.

Ironically, the Bible itself is written with a bravehearted voice. Read it afresh, and if you are willing to hear it, there is a relentless pressure that the words of Scripture place upon the soul. Jesus didn't just give hugs; He also gave a hammer. Paul didn't just pass on holy kisses; he also tirelessly dealt out swift and holy kicks to the rear end of the ancient church. The Bible has the manly stuff intact, and that is why it is such a great mystery how it got lost in the modern church.

The bravehearted path is all about life—*abundant life*. But you cannot experience the fullness of that abundant life if you're all hugs and no hammers.

There are books that are weighty with high-minded intellectualism that sound impressive but often bring little life to the soul. This book is, I hope, a smart book, but it won't try and sound smart. This book isn't out to impress you, but rather, to press you into the arms of the manly side of Christ's grace. This book is a shot of adrenaline to the spiritual life—*literally*. It's an introduction to the long-forgotten manly side of truth. And trust me, when you see this manly side in action, you will marvel. It is strong, heroic, noble, brave, and ravishingly handsome—it's the lion-side of Jesus Christ brought back to the center stage of Christianity. And it's not just for men, it's for everyone—both young and old, male and female. It's simply Christ, the way He actually is.

Part Three

CURB APPEAL

Silicone saints and botoxed believers

Nine

The Secret Sauce

Beware: This chapter contains the word *cool*. I have been warned by my younger constituency that such a word is used only by people who are wholly uncool. But as you will see in the upcoming pages of this book, being uncool might not be such a bad thing after all.

———

Cool Christians—they seem to be everywhere nowadays. Yes, I realize that, according to the words of Christ and almost 2000 years of history, becoming a Christian has traditionally meant being rejected, persecuted, and despised, a life dead to this world and its applause. But there is quite a powerful host amongst the rank and file today who are laboring to change this definition. After all, it is a bit dour and unattractive, and because Christianity needs to try and keep up with the growing forces of Islam, it seems we need to give Jesus' image a little makeover and pump a lot more moola into the marketing and publicity coffers of the church and a little less into the dead-to-sin and dead-to-this-world department.

For the sake of our conversation, let's define coolness:

> Coolness is the measurement of favor you curry from the world, society, and your peers and is the gradient of attraction that you hold in the eyes of those who value the things of this earth.

In other words, Jesus wasn't cool.

But I've got some ear-tingling good news. Even though He wasn't, it now appears that *we can be*.

We all know the world can be cool, but it seems, according to recent discoveries, that the church can be cool, too! And if you're wondering how you too can become a cool Christian, I'm going to give you everything you need to succeed in the corridors of modern Christianity.

Here's the secret recipe:

First, you must be avant-garde in your thinking. You can't be predictable in your theology and doctrine—nothing old-fashioned will do. You need to have fresh thoughts about Jesus, about what He said, and about what He is wanting us to do. Reinvent the gospel, redefine its key words, and reform its entire intent. People will love it, your books will sell, and you will look very cool in the process.

Second, you have to have a sense of style. No Donald Trump hairdos allowed. You need to make sure that you package yourself in attire that will woo the crowds, stimulate talk, and beckon interest in who you are. Show a little underwear, a little more skin, a little less modesty. Send out a strong message that *you* are not boring or legalistic. Bring some serious attitude with your presentation, and make sure everyone knows that you are not just a follower of trends, but a maker of trends.

Third, you mustn't sound too pure in your speech. You need to add a little coarseness in here and there. It is currently in vogue to startle your listeners with a little profanity just to let them know that you aren't some old-timey moralistic crusader. Butchering grammar can be an effective way to prove that you are not too straight-laced and formal, but just make sure you do it in a cool-sounding way. Oh, and talking about crude and disgusting things in the context of Christianity wins serious points with your audience.

Fourth, it really helps if you are a bit tipsy on the weekends and can be associated with alcohol or tobacco in some measure. For studies have shown that it is effective for your coolness in Christianity if you stretch those antiquated moral boundaries for the sake of the gospel. After all, no one is interested in joining the church if it's a temperance society.[1]

Oh, and fifth, the coolest of the cool Christians today are certified and self-acknowledged cynics of the Word of God, Jesus Christ, and everyone who dares to bear His name. I call it Vogue Doubt, and let me tell you, it wins massive cool points with the modern Christian establishment. The more you question what everyone else accepts, even if it is true, the more you'll sound like one of those angsty artistic types who are especially avant-garde.

Sixth, if you are going to be cool in your Christianity, you have to know the jargon. There are certain cool words you can use to describe your beliefs (or your lack thereof): *systemic, coherent, contextual, conversational, comprehensive, generative, missional, postmodern*—and throw in the word *ecumenical,* and you will get a lot of smiles and pats on the back. The weird thing is, quite often, people don't care if you know what these words all mean. They just sound really good coming off the tongue.

PRESENTATION, IMITATION, AND ABDICATION

I spent 19 years of my life attempting to be a cool Christian. I'm sure I duped a few along the way, but overall, I'd guess that most people who know me are fairly confident in my normalcy and my total lack of coolness. I don't use cool vocabulary, I don't have my own cool style, I don't participate in any shockingly cool morality-busting activities, I don't have that cool Vogue Doubt, and I don't lace my books with cool profanity to prove that the gospel has set me free. I'm starting to get a bit depressed as I make this list—I mean, I knew I wasn't cool, but I didn't realize that I was ridiculously plain.

If you missed the first section of this book, I'm a 36-year-old guy who, the other day, was mistaken for being a 16-year-old (I'm not kidding; it really happened). So for all practical purposes, I should be still trying to be cool. After all, if people think I'm 16, I should probably at least try and woo the crowds as if I am. But I gave up on the cool pursuit nearly 17 years ago. Oh, I've still had my flare-ups along the way, like the time I bought those blue jeans with all the manufacturer-induced rips and black stains on them (name me one good reason why someone should buy a pair of pants for $63 that have rips and stains all over them). There is definitely a part of all of us that wishes to be deemed vogue or hip by society, and I must admit I'm not immune to the temptation.

One thing I must make clear, however: I didn't trade in my coolness for dullness. Actually, I traded in my coolness for something far better than a "cool" Christianity, which usually just ends up being a poor imitation of the world's latest fad anyway. Forgive me for not divulging right now what exactly I traded up for, but I'll do my best to explain it to you as we venture forward in this book. A little hint: It's not something overly simplistic like, "I traded in my coolness for Jesus."

Now just to remind you, this book is about jamming that manly stuff back into the body of Christ. And to do that, we are going to have to go into all the little crevices that are crammed full of anti-masculine sentiment and do a little cleaning. This whole cool thing is just one small arena.

Now, just to forewarn you, we are quickly approaching another awkward moment. There is absolutely no way around the political incorrectness of this statement, so I'm just going to say it: The widespread preoccupation among Christians with being in vogue, in style, and cool is an evidence of an out-of-balance feminine emphasis on beauty and allure in the modern Christian mentality.

I know, I know, that was not a socially polished statement. My buddy Ben thought I should have worded it as follows: The widespread preoccupation among Christians with being in vogue, in style, and cool is an evidence of the *emasculation* of the modern church.

Yes, that sounds more proper, but it's really just another way of saying that when the manly stuff is missing, all that is left to be observed is the feminine side of the equation.

As I stated earlier, I am in no way seeking a return to an exclusively masculine rendition of Christianity. When the masculine emphasis dominates the Christian mentality, you often end up with dour faces and long, shapeless gray dresses. Remember, I'm not criticizing femininity. Rather, I'm criticizing the effects of a worldview and approach to the Christian life that excludes the balancing presence of the manly stuff.

So, back to my statement: The widespread preoccupation among Christians with being in vogue, in style, and cool is an evidence of an out-of-balance feminine emphasis on beauty and allure in the modern Christian mentality.

Take a man and a woman, give them each $1000, and set them both loose on a shopping spree. In a figuratypic sense[1] the man heads to Home Depot and shores up his toolbox, and the woman heads to the mall and shores up her closet. The masculine drive is toward functionality, while the feminine impetus is towards beauty and allure. Neither are incorrect in and of themselves, but if one purposely excludes the other you end up with poorly decorated bachelor pads on one side and gaudy credit card debt on the other.

When it comes to the alluring presentation of anything, whether it be a home, an event, or even something as simple as one's clothing, women are generally better at it than men. Women seem to have an inbuilt emphasis toward beauty and allure that is seriously lacking in most guys that haven't yet gotten in touch with their feminine side. While this emphasis on beauty and allure is hard at work scouring the local mall for just the right accessory, the straightforward masculine emphasis who has been dragged along to accompany her spies a bargain bin, snatches up the much-sought-after item, and exclaims, "Here's a belt!" which is just as quickly followed up with a hopeful, "Can we go now?"

When it comes to an alluring presentation, most men just don't get it. For a lot of guys the entire point of clothing is to simply not be naked when you leave the house. And whereas it is obvious that men, the church, and society have a *lot* to gain from this feminine emphasis on beauty and allure, it is also true that women, the church, and society have just as much to gain from the often liberating masculine emphasis on unashamed, unassuming, straightforward presentation.

Things, for the most part, are no different when it comes to the presentation of the gospel. The feminine emphasis is toward a beautiful and alluring presentation. The manly emphasis, on the other hand, is toward an unashamed, unassuming, and straightforward presentation. Men, in a figuratypic sense, spend far less time on their appearance than do women. The fact that women spend more time on their appearance than men do is, of course, not a bad thing, but when the feminine emphasis loses the balance of the manly side it ends up with an unhealthy overemphasis on being fashionable. Meanwhile, the manly emphasis without the feminine side to balance it out ends up with an overemphasis on functionality and becomes dour and austere as a result. What the church and this dying world need are beauty *and* unashamed straightforwardness. That is what the combination of a man and woman bring about—poetic strength, dignified passion, noble etiquette, and the unvarnished truth spoken with love and wonder. But as long as we maintain our seemingly exclusive preoccupation with beauty and allure at the expense of speaking strong and straight, we will never find this beautiful and majestic balance. We need to bring back the manly stuff.

The attention given to this whole cool Christian thing turns my stomach. Part of me wants to laugh at all this ridiculousness, but then when I think about the fact that these self-appointed "cool dudes" are messing with the gospel and the very people whom Christ purchased with His blood, it riles me up.

Go to your local Christian bookstore and study the music CD covers. Try not to laugh as you stack these album covers against my "recipe for coolness" and see how many of these artists are playing the "I'm really cool" game. Every once in a while you stumble across an album cover that has a nice smiling face without even a hint of pretension (thank God for these!), but for the most part we have some serious evidences of "I've got the look, don't I?" Now this doesn't necessarily mean that these artists' hearts aren't pure and their music isn't pleasing to God, but it does show how this feminine emphasis on presentation and allure has become deeply ingrained in the fiber of the modern church. (Note: I have a few past book and album covers of my own that deserve a little snicker of derision, so don't think I'm excluding even myself from this investigation.)

Another interesting research project I would encourage (I'm not sure *encourage* is the correct word), is to attend one of the annual Youth Specialties youth worker conferences. Spend a few days with today's youth workers and you will spy out more than a fair share of "cool dudes" in the mix. Youth work has a very infectious case of this "cool" disease. It spreads like gangrene throughout the youth pastoral system and pretty soon every single one of the male leaders has highlights in his hair and every female leader has a pierced belly button. (Note: I myself have worked with Christian youth for over 12 years, and though I never attempted to highlight my hair, I did buy that tattered $63 pair of ultra-hip pants. So again, I'm not immune to this critique.)

Oh, and before I forget, let me give you one more thing to check into. Peruse an emergent Christian book. Just look at the top of the Christian bestsellers list and you are sure to find a few to choose from. If you don't know how to find one, just ask the person behind the counter at the local Christian bookstore—he is sure to know. These open-mind philosophical treatises are loaded with the cool gene. They have plenty of both the allure and the presentation that people want to hear. They have the look, the cynicism, the angst, the crudeness, and even the style.

Just don't expect to find any straightforwardness within the pages. These books are classic examples of a Christianity that's missing the manly stuff. (Note: Much to the chagrin of the emergent church movement, this book very possibly will be classified as emergent—it rocks the boat, asks the tough questions, and stirs people up—but I'm hoping it will be one of the first emergent books to actually pull it off with biblical truth intact.)

The cool issue in the body of Christ is one of those things that you may just smile wryly at and view as just an odd piece of the modern religious tapestry of Christian expression. After all, who really cares if these guys are just overgrown teenagers curiously preoccupied with beauty and allure? But my issue with it stems a bit deeper than beauty and allure. For years I've stood by and watched what this cool emphasis has done to truth, and I just can't stand by and stay silent any longer.

Eleven

METROTHEISM

I have a friend who, for the sake of anonymity, we will refer to as Metro. I have known Metro for well over eight years and have watched him go from serious, conservative, home-schooled, Christian male to something altogether bewildering. Oh, he's still a professing Christian. In fact, he is a semi-influential Christian. But he and his Christianity have gone funky and even absurd.

There is no doubt that Metro is a cool Christian. He has a cool way of talking, a cool way of walking, and even a cool way of singing into the microphone at concerts. Did I forget to mention that Metro is a musician?

Metro has found the "freedom in Christ" to be tipsy on the weekends while jesting with the bar crowd about crude and distasteful things. In fact, this has become his form of evangelism. He works bar gigs on the weekends, singing his mournful melodies for the inebriated. His songs aren't even Christian songs, but as I understand it, the strategy behind the bar gigs isn't to "preach at them" but to "love them with my eyes."

- Metro believes Jesus Christ is God in the flesh.
- Metro believes that Jesus Christ is his personal Savior.
- Metro believes the Bible is inspired, at least to a point.
- Metro even believes that he is forgiven and that he is loved by his Father in heaven.

Metro passes all the spiritual tests our modern Christian world has established. He's a bona fide Christian according to our modern system. But it is difficult to find a life more opposite of Jesus Christ's.

- Metro is self-centered and egotistical. Life is all about him, his career, his look, his image.
- Metro is ruled by his flesh. So whatever his appetite craves, he believes he is free to indulge in.
- Metro is an absolute wimp. If you want to know what he believes, you will have to drag it out of him.
- Metro is all about beauty and allure.

Metro is a guy, but Metro wears makeup. Not just for his bar gigs, but for everyday life. He also wears girls' jeans, and is more interested in shoes than any 20 of my man friends combined. Now don't get me wrong; he isn't homosexual. Metro is married and is, as far as I know, happily heterosexual. But for me, Metro is almost too perfect an illustration of what has happened to modern-day Christianity. It's gone girly, not just outwardly, but inwardly.

Even though Metro is a male, his presentation of himself as well as the gospel is decidedly feminine in emphasis. This choice is a very deliberate one. It is calculated and it is derived from a very "open mind, touchy feely" worldview that would rather entice people into the church than inform about truth. As I said, Metro is all about beauty and allure. He is startlingly feminine not only in his dress, but in his beliefs and in his Christianity. And if Metro's look is to be defined as metrosexual, then his overly feminized take on Christianity is a position that I would call *metrotheism*.

I love my friend Metro. I really do. But I have no stomach for him traipsing around like a drag queen under the banner of Jesus Christ. This new metrosexual look may be wildly popular, and the new metrotheistic church may pack out the pews, but neither woos anyone to the cross. The cross has no place in metrotheistic churches. There's nothing even remotely alluring about it. Marketing and presentation aside, the fact remains that Jesus died covered in blood hanging naked between two thieves. This leaves a bit of a public relations issue for the modern church. Metrotheism is so preoccupied with beauty and allure in order to entice people through entertainment and comfort that it misses the entire point of the gospel. Not only is it missing the point, but it is missing the power that only an unashamed, unassuming, straightforward presentation of the gospel can bring. And I strongly believe it is hindering the truth and obscuring the reality of Jesus Christ.

Metrotheism has, in many ways, saturated the modern church. We are obsessed with our presentation and our appearance. We've been so concerned about being cool, relevant, and fun that we have forgotten to be bread, light, and life to a hungry, dark, and dying world. We have forgotten that we are not here to make people feel more comfortable about themselves and their time spent inside of a church building. That is simply not what Christianity is about. Christianity is about a kingdom, a glory, a power, a love, a grace, a righteousness, an eternal triumph, and yielding to the all-powerful King who is bringing it all about.

Metrotheism is cool Christianity. It's "just be real" Christianity. It's an "open-minded" Christianity. And it is a Christianity that carries around vogue doubt as if it were a forged driver's license enabling its holder to buy beer at the age of 12. Oh, and metrotheism is also supremely impotent and powerless to effect even the slightest change in the soul for God. It's defeated, and proud of its defeat.

As Christians we often think of atheists as the arch-nemesis of the church. But I would propose that metrotheism is as grand of an opponent as the church may have ever encountered. And the reason I consider it such a formidable opponent is due to the fact that it is not standing outside the gates of Christendom attempting to get in, but it is actually in charge of the majority of the Christian system today. And this metrotheism isn't just in our leaders, our books, and our music. It's even crept into our doctrine, and to some degree, it's in *all of us*. And the manly man in me is saying, "It's high time for this metroridiculousness to adios!"

Twelve

DRESSING UP JESUS

L et's come back to our definition of coolness:

> Coolness is the measurement of favor you curry from the world, society, and your peers and is the gradient of attraction that you hold in the eyes of those who value the things of this earth.

As I stated earlier, Jesus wasn't cool. But what I think we don't understand very well is that this uncoolness wasn't incidental or accidental—it was by design.

The Bible says that God *chose* the foolish (uncool) things of this world purposely to confound the wise, and the weak things of this world in order to frustrate the strong, and the things that were nothing to bring to nothing those things which everyone thought to be everything.[1] Do we realize that He *chose* these things? And that He chose these things *on purpose?*

What does it mean when the God of the Ages chooses to come to Earth as a baby in a manger instead of a prince in a palace? The thought boggles the mind. It staggers me to think that the High and Holy One of Heaven chose to be born of a virgin, which for all practical purposes brought Him into this world looking like an illegitimate child. He chose to be born in Nazareth, of which it was said, no good thing can come out of.[2] It shames my ego, which is constantly clamoring for more, to know that the One who owns the cattle on a thousand hills chose poverty instead of wealth. The Famous One chose obscurity over popularity, and the Almighty chose weakness in place of strength. He came as a servant instead of a king. He entered Jerusalem on a donkey instead of on a stallion. He commanded a small band of uneducated fishermen and others instead of wielding a scepter over legions of angels. And last, but by no means least, He died the death of a condemned criminal, stripped naked between two thieves, so that I could breathe the fresh air of freedom.

He chose this. He chose it on purpose. And then He said to you and me, "Come and follow."[3]

Maybe Jesus just didn't know about being a cool Christian and how effective of a witnessing tool it can be. Maybe He didn't know about all the people He could have reached if He would have only related to them in a style that oozed beauty and allure from every pore.

But I doubt it.

The Lamb was slain from before the foundation of the world. And God planned every detail of His advent on Earth down to the very last jot and tittle. He knew what He was doing. And He knew what He was choosing.

Isaiah 53 prophesied that Jesus would have "no form nor comeliness," and that "when we shall see him, there is no beauty that we should desire him."

That doesn't sound very cool. But that is exactly what God chose. And He chose it to make a point.

He chose poverty to prove that a man's life does not consist of the abundance of the things that he possesses.

He chose weakness to prove that it is not by might nor by power but by the Spirit of Almighty God that men are made and battles won.

He chose obscurity to prove that it profits a man nothing if he should gain the whole world and lose his own soul.

He chose the path that men deemed foolish to prove that God's ways are not our ways and that our ways are not God's ways. And that, in fact, God's ways are higher than man's as the heavens are higher than the Earth.

He chose the path that was despised to prove that blessed are those of whom all men speak evil for righteousness's sake, for they walk in the company of the prophets, the martyrs, and in the footsteps of the very Son of God.

And finally, He chose death to prove that all those who seek to save their life will lose it, but those who will release their grip on life for the glory of God and the proclamation of His kingdom will without doubt gain it in the end. For truly, they can never die.[4]

We know what He chose. But what are *we* choosing?

They call us Christians; and all that really means is that we are supposed to follow Christ.

The question is...are we?

There is a simple truth in the kingdom of God: The more beautiful and stunning you are to this world, the more disagreeable you are in the eyes of Heaven. Or the inverse could be stated: The more lovely you are to heaven, the more disagreeable you will, by nature, be in the eyes of this world. Heaven and Earth represent two contrary systems and they are at odds one with the other.

It never ceases to amaze me why any of us as Christians ever spend even a moment's time considering what this world thinks about us (or what it thinks about anything, for that matter). But in our never-ending attempt to be cool, most of us don't just consider what the world thinks. We often go to great lengths to imitate it, letting it define our behavior, shape our doctrine, and even affect our presentation of what we believe.

A.W. Tozer puts it this way:

> A great deal can be learned about people by observing whom and what they imitate. The weak, for instance, imitate the strong; never the reverse. The poor imitate the rich. The self-assured are imitated by the timid and uncertain, the genuine is imitated by the counterfeit, and people all tend to imitate what they admire.
>
> By this definition power today lies with the world, not with the church, for it is the world that initiates and the church that imitates what she has initiated. By this definition the church admires the world. The church is uncertain and looks to the world for assurance. A weak church is aping a strong world to the amusement of intelligent sinners and to her own everlasting shame.[5]

It's one thing to bring shame upon ourselves; but it is another thing entirely to bring shame upon the name of Jesus.

What has happened to the church? Do the holy angels look down and sadly shake their heads to find us worshiping wantonly at the feet of culture instead of at the feet of Christ? The cool mind is a renegade running free within the modern church system due largely to the fact that we have lost our concern over what Heaven thinks. Instead, the bride of Christ is gazing longingly toward the world, toward its universities, toward its fashion magazines, towards its culturally refined personalities, as she asks with shifting feet and uncertain stance, "How do I look? Do you like me? Do you want me? Do you approve?" These seem to be the questions foremost on our mind. And like a lonely teenage girl hungry for love, it would appear that we are willing to do almost anything to get the answers we most want to hear.

We are supposed to be a people who live only for the adoration and attention of that One who loved us, even unto death. And yet lately it seems that we have been panting with desire for the affection of others.

Affection isn't hard to get. If a girl plays to a guy's lusts, she'll get plenty of it. But she's selling herself short, and in the end, *she* is the one that's being used.

It is a simple fact: The world has never played hard to get. All the church has ever had to do to move from curses to kisses is turn up the beauty and allure and give people exactly what they want.

For instance, here's a great recipe for a really cool megachurch:

- Become more like the world so that the world will be attracted.
- Take out all the hard-hammer truths so that the world won't be offended.
- Make overtures toward universalism, relativism, and ecumenicalism so that the world can be impressed.
- Dress up Jesus a bit to make Him seem more like a kind friend rather than the King of kings and Lord of lords so that the world might find Him more agreeable.

How have we missed the point that if Jesus was interested in impressing the world He would have approached His coming in an entirely different way? Jesus flunked the cool test and it didn't bother Him. In fact, He seems to have gone out of His way to be despised by this world, its systems, and its institutions. So why are we pandering to them?

The cool mind is altering the face of Christianity. It's literally plastic surgery on the body of Christ. I mean, let's admit it: Jesus, the way He is in the Bible, is a little bit uncomfortable. So let's dress Him up a tad, change the shape of His nose, fix that gap between His two front teeth, shave off that beard, spritz Him with a little flowery perfume, and then retranslate all His words into a modern vernacular so that we can delete all His harsh phraseology without anyone realizing that we're doing it.

And the whole while, we think we are helping people find their Savior, when in actuality, we are merely introducing them to an impostor of our own making—an imaginary, impotent metro-Jesus wearing makeup and girls' pants. No one is actually meeting the Master of the Worlds Himself—the Rider on the white steed who wears many crowns upon His majestic brow, has a sword protruding from His mouth, is clothed in a vesture dipped in blood, and bears the words *King of kings and Lord of lords* on His right thigh.[6]

The world doesn't need just another frail friend. It needs a mighty Savior.

When you empty truth of its manly stuff, you end up with weak, harmless, froufrou ideas that sound good but offer absolutely no power to change human life. Christianity historically has been set apart from all other world religions in the fact that it actually offers power, life, joy, peace, and victory and not merely a long list of rules, ceremonies, and sacrificial rites.

Christianity is actually supposed to *work.* It is supposed to have power to perform and implement a supernatural overhaul within the human body and soul. This is the reason it is so profound and controversial. But modern Christianity, last time I looked, isn't working so well. There is no power (at least not in North America). Instead, there is marginal life, mediocre amounts of joy, shaky peace, and little to no victory over sin. Something is broken. And something needs to be fixed, but all the mechanically minded fix-it-upper men are currently ashamed of their God-given abilities and emphases so they're all attempting to address these gargantuan problems not with the tools that God gave them, but with an understanding hug and a listening ear.

The cool mind, with its supersensitivity to public opinion polls and popularity ratings, has unwittingly begun to alter the historic moorings of Christian truth in an attempt to make the truth of Christ more palatable to our degenerate culture.

For instance, *the gospel* has been reduced to a message merely about forgiveness while the idea of regeneration and transformation seems almost totally forgotten. *Grace* has become simply a gigantic hug from God and is no longer the muscle of God brought to earth to aid the weakness of men and to give them strength. *Faith* has morphed into this bizarre idea of "honest doubt" and has lost its essence of rock-solid unwavering confidence in the ability of God to perform that which He promises. *Holiness* has transformed into moralistic tyranny for the soul and something to be avoided at all costs. *Righteousness* has been redefined to mean an unreachable standard of perfection. *Purity* has become nothing more than a legalistic attempt to stay away from things and thoughts that God knows we won't be able to abstain from anyway. *Love* has become unconditional acceptance and tolerance of sin. The list goes on and on. In our desperate attempt at dressing up Jesus to make both us and Him more appealing to the cool crowd, the simple beauty of truth has somehow become lost under all the pretension and makeup.

The integrity of everything Christ came to accomplish and provide for His bride is hanging woefully in the balance, and there is hardly even a whisper these days about the travesty. If there was ever a time for fixer men and women, warrior men and women, truth-protecting men and women to rise up and do something, *it is now.*

THE BRAVEHEARTED PATH

CONTRA MUNDUM

I fully accept the fact that some of you are going to love this brave-hearted path and some of you are going to hate it. Believe me, I won't take it personally if this stuff is causing you to think nasty things about me. Unfortunately, this gritty gospel blueprint has created controversy in every generation, and those who choose to "bring it" have a long and painful history of stonings, crucifixions, loss of limbs, burnings, imprisonments, and feedings to lions. So, because I'm rather new at this, please try not to bring out the chair, duct tape, and torture devices at least until I release my second book on the subject.

Now there aren't too many people around these days that can read Latin, but if you could, you might pick up on the vibe of where this particular section of the bravehearted path is going.

Contra mundum.

Whereas those two words might possibly be new to you, they have a long and glorious history in the world of the bravehearted saints. And, you have to admit, there is just something about Latin phraseology that makes life seem more noble, dignified, and adventurous.

Well, enough small talk—let's get down to business!

There is a story in Christian history that I'm surprised hasn't yet been turned into either a novel or a movie. Maybe it already has, and in my "movie fast" I just happened to miss it. But this story is good—it's full of pithy irony, it includes a violent clash between strong personalities, and the drama is of the life-and-death variety.

I'm not going to try to present you with the novelesque version of it here; I'll leave that for someone else to do. But I will try to give you a brief overview of the situation.

The Scene: Saxony, Germany—1517

The Players: Martin Luther and Desiderius Erasmus

The Situation: The Christian church has gone apostate. The Word of God is no longer central and no longer authoritative in the midst of the church. People are no longer turning to Jesus Christ for salvation, but have resorted to buying their way, with cold hard cash, out of sin and into heaven. The leaders are corrupt, the truth is lost, and the whole thing is a wreck. But on the other hand the church is, for lack of a more historic sounding description…*very cool.* It has loads of money from all the indulgences being sold, and so its cathedrals are magnificent, jewel-laden monoliths showcasing the most striking forms of beauty and allure money can buy. As I said, *very cool.*

Act One: Introducing Desiderius Erasmus, the ultimate people person, diplomat, and friend. Everyone loves Erasmus; he is kindhearted, soft-spoken, and a true gentleman. He's not only one of the most brilliant men in the entire church system, but he's one of those guys who knows how to make you smile and feel important. Erasmus is a true scholar and a God-fearing man.

Erasmus, in his study of Scripture, becomes convinced that the church, in the year 1517, is not just off, it's *way off.* So Erasmus begins the process of change. He figures he will begin to appeal to those "in the know" and try to woo them into a more biblical way of thinking. His ideas are radical, but his method is so unassuming and gentle that he begins to win a few adherents. In fact, one of his adherents is a man named Martin Luther.

Act Two: Introducing Martin Luther, the ultimate thunderbolt—brash, and daring as a silver spoon diving into a monastery's garbage disposal. Luther is as courageous as they come, as honest as Abe, and an all-out advocate of the God of the universe. He's not as smart as Erasmus, but he's also not an idiot. And what he lacks in brains he makes up for in sheer guts. Maybe Luther isn't the most likeable guy around, but you can't knock his gumption.

While Erasmus is ever-so-slowly attempting to relationally win over the leadership of the church, Luther begins a different sort of campaign all on his own. A bit disturbed by Erasmus's lack of results and his softy techniques for delivering the truth of the gospel, Luther decides to write up a little letter on a piece of parchment and nail it up to the Wittenberg door.

Act Three: It turns out Luther's letter wasn't just a "Hi! How you are doing today?" sort of letter. In fact, it draws fire and brimstone down from the Pope himself. After all, how would you like it if one of your subordinates proclaimed to the entire world that the company you were managing was basically corrupt and of the devil? His letter was audacious, brash, foolhardy, and worthy of a hundred other unseemly adjectives. Never mind the fact that what Luther wrote was all true—you just aren't supposed to say things like that, especially about the Pope! It's just not cool.

And this is where all the drama kicks into full gear. For in the process of Luther being brought before the powers that be and chastised as a heretic, dismissed as a maniac, and cursed as a devilish dissenter, Luther decides to take this opportunity to mention his allies and clarify that he isn't the only one who feels this way. And right then and there out pops the name Desiderius Erasmus.

Act Four: Erasmus, the diplomat and politician that he was, immediately distanced himself from this crazy German known as Luther. I can just hear him now: "Luther? Never heard of him!"

When Luther hears that Erasmus has dismissed his antics as basically rebellious and extreme, Luther sighs incredulously and pronounces to the entire church at large that Erasmus is a coward.

Act Five: The rest is for the history books. Luther goes on to lead what modern history knows as the Protestant Reformation of the church, while Erasmus proved to be his most venomous opponent. It may very well be accurate to say that no one in the Catholic Church opposed the Reformation more than the man who inspired it in the first place.[1]

Good story, huh? Well, it wasn't for the story's sake that I told it, but I hope you enjoyed it. I wanted to pass on this story because it has personally helped me articulate some things that have been stirring around inside my heart for many years.

You see, there are two kinds of men in this story. A girly sort of man, Erasmus, and a burly sort of man, Luther. Both have their problems. Erasmus is so concerned about the beauty and allure of his message and about what people think of him that he distances himself from the truth of his message at the first sign of combat, while Luther is so impatient, headstrong, and focused on the straightforward presentation of truth that he is willing to denounce everyone and everything that doesn't see things his way at first glance.

Both of these men had the truth, but neither of them handled it with the loving and majestic dexterity of Jesus Christ. One was too soft, the other one was too hard. Now don't get me wrong—I'm a huge fan of the Reformation. I'm just not a very big fan of how some of it was pulled off. You see, I have a theory that I've been nursing for quite a few years. For instance, what might have happened if the alluring Erasmus had united forces with the straightforward Luther and they had approached this whole thing with a little more of the bravehearted sort of flair? What if Luther had lent an ear to Erasmus and allowed some of his holy grit to be polished until it shone with the allure of Heaven? And what if Erasmus had lent an ear to Luther and allowed some of his alluring presentation to be replaced with swift kicks and proclamations? Could it be that the church could have still reformed and brought back Jesus Christ and the Word of God to the center stage without the need of a gruesome 131-year religious war and countless lives being butchered and tormented in the process?

You see, I've always been an Erasmus. I'm one of those guys who says, "Let's make appeals, let's talk it out, let's give it a little more time to heal." When I study Erasmus in history, it's sort of like staring at myself in the mirror, minus his high IQ, of course. As of five years ago, I didn't have even a smidgen of Luther in my blood. In fact, Luther's blunt brashness has always been somewhat offensive to my "girly" sensibilities. I've always been a lover and not a fighter. And then God began to acquaint me with the bravehearted path. Come to find out, the bravehearted path isn't Erasmus. And strangely, it's also not Luther. It seems to be the mixture of the two. It's Erasmus–Luther all combined into one extraordinary presentation of truth.

I remember about four years ago when I got up the guts to pray, "God, stick more Luther in my blood!" Boy, watch out what you pray for! This bravehearted path has dramatically altered me. There are probably some of you who might think I'm a lot more Luther than Erasmus after reading the first two sections of this book. The girly-to-burly balance has definitely come into a greater equilibrium within these past few years. And yes, there have been moments when I've asked God to make sure I don't go flying off the scales in the Luther direction. I don't want to be an *Erasm*ian shmuck, but I also don't want to be a *Luther*ian hockey puck to the teeth.

Jesus was the perfect example of the bravehearted balance. He was the perfect blend of strength and grace. He was the ultimate warrior-poet. He was inwardly as strong as a lion, but also miraculously as sensitive as a lamb. He knew when to flex His muscles and when to endure the cross without even whispering a word in His own defense. He is the Bridegroom in the Song of Songs as well as the Rider on the White Steed in Revelation 19. And, without equivocation, this is what I want to become as well.

The modern church has become very much anti-*Luther*ian in its sensibilities. We are attracted like moths to the flame of Erasmus's kind-hearted sermons. But, kindhearted sermons won't erase the decay of modern doctrine, they won't repeal the doubting trajectory of the contemporary soul, they won't kick out the cool dudes and the cool minds in our midst, and they won't turn this colossal ship called Christianity around. We need a massive kick in the shorts—we need a Luther-like call to issue forth within the corridors of the modern church. We need another letter pinned to the Wittenberg door. We need men to start barking out things like, "If I had a thousand heads I would rather have them all cut off than to revoke!"[2] And even though it may not be cool, we need the manly stuff jammed back into the Christian faith.

There is one bravehearted sort of fellow in Christian history whom I've always really liked. He possessed a more unashamed, unassuming, and straightforward presentation than Erasmus, and yet more beauty and allure than Luther. His name was Athanasius. This guy was a warrior-poet through and through. And like Luther, he took on the religious establishment of his day in order to preserve the soundness of truth.

All throughout Christian history, Satan has been laboring 24/7 to sneak error into the church. And back in Athanasius's day, it was no different. Back in the fourth century, there was a guy named Arius who was militantly marketing the idea that Jesus wasn't actually God. And this Arius guy was a smooth talker. He was cool, and he was winning powerful leaders over to his viewpoint by the droves. For Athanasius, this was serious business—this was all about the glory of God in Jesus Christ. For Jesus was the Creator of all existence come to earth in the body of a man!

Athanasius defended the full deity of Jesus Christ against emperors, magistrates, bishops, and theologians. The guy was considered so uncool that he was banished five times.[3] This fellow was willing to put it all on the line for Jesus Christ even against the most powerful forces in the world. I love it! I love this bravehearted stuff! It's valiant, it's noble, it's honorable, and it's daring even in the face of death!

Look at this description of Athanasius by Saint Gregory the Great, who lived in the sixth century A.D. Just think about a warrior-poet as you read these words:

> (Athanasius) was sublime in action, lowly in mind; inaccessible in virtue, most accessible in conversation; gentle, free from anger, sympathetic, sweet in words, sweeter in disposition; angelic in appearance, more angelic in mind; calm in rebuke, persuasive in praise, without spoiling the good effect of either by excess, but rebuking with the tenderness of a father...[4]

This is the bravehearted path. This is the kind of substance that has caused the Christian faith to endure throughout the many generations of genocide and persecution. It's not just long-suffering love and mercy, but stalwart unyielding loyalty to the integrity of the gospel as handed down throughout the centuries.

The well-known statement throughout Christian history is "Athanasius *contra mundum*." It's a Latin phrase that means, "Athanasius against the world." I have repeated that singular statement over and over to myself since I first heard it nearly 18 years ago. I always picture Athanasius standing before Emperor Constantine and all the legions of Arian loyalists, proclaiming at the top of his voice, "Here I stand— I will yield not!"

Then I picture Constantine saying, "The entire world is against you, Athanasius! Will you not recant?"

Then I see Athanasius stare back at Constantine and declare, "If the world stands against me, then Athanasius is against the world!" (If this were a movie, the music score would certainly swell to a climax at this precise point.)

To be willing to be *contra mundum*, to be willing to be against the world, is not the cool thing to do, but it is the very essence of historic, biblical Christianity. To be willing to stand like William Wilberforce against slavery when all of Parliament barks with fury to drown out your singular voice is the stuff of the bravehearted. To be willing to stand like John Knox and proclaim amidst the heat of the fiercest persecution, "I fear not the tyranny of man, neither yet what the devil can invent against me,"[5] is the type of boldness that Satan doesn't know how to handle. To be willing to stand like Luther when Pope Leo is screaming in your face that you will be consigned to hell if you don't recant—now *that's* the manly stuff!

We often think of such opposition as being the stuff of movies and not real life. But if we were to be honest about the battle for truth within our very own souls, there is a need for the spirit of *contra mundum* to be alive within our inner beings every day, even every moment.

Doubt barks, "This isn't true, this can't be true, this whole Christian thing is a lie!"

But the miniature, ever-growing Athanasius within us cries out, "Here I stand!"

Hollywood scoffs, "Your faith is hollow. It's based upon mythologies and fables!"

But the miniature, ever-growing Luther within us cries out, "Here I stand!"

Our friends mock, "This is just a phase you're going through. One day you will see this whole Christian thing for what it is—a mere psychological elixir!"

But the miniature, ever-growing Wilberforce within us cries out, "Here I stand!"

Even the modern church chimes in: "Now, be careful not to expect too much from God in this life. Otherwise you will end up disappointed and disillusioned and forsake your faith altogether."

But the miniature, ever-growing Jesus Christ within us cries out, "Here I stand!"

This world will do whatever it can to refute the idea of Jesus Christ, the idea of faith, the idea of the gospel. But the bravehearted spirit is a fighting spirit—bendable by grace, but unbending to the enemies of grace.

When the manly stuff enters back into the church, then the spirit of *contra mundum* is stoked within the hearth of the body of Christ once again. But God is desiring His church to be *contra mundum* not just with abrasive thunder, but with the heavenly combination of a lion and a lamb. And such is the brilliance of the bravehearted path.

The following is an autobiographical statement made by Luther about himself:

> I am rough, boisterous, stormy, and altogether warlike. I am born to fight against innumerable monsters and devils. I must remove stumps and stones, cut away thistles and thorns, and clear the wild forests.[6]

We need to pray for more Luther-like thunder to be injected back into the body of Christ. I realize that if we add back in too much Luther we might become a rather scary bunch. But as long as we continue to nurture only our *Erasmi*an sensibilities, and continue to push away this rough and warlike substance, the very truth of the gospel is at danger from a thousand different foes both in our individual lives and in the life of the church.

Our God does not seek to be cool. He does not attempt to curry favor with this world like the politicians of our day. He does not pander after the good opinion of men like an attention-starved little puppy. Our God deeply longs for the people of this world to know Him and entrust their lives to Him. But He will not compromise His truth, in even the slightest way, in order to win His bride.

Our God is *contra mundum*. He isn't in step with this world—rather, He is contrary to it. He isn't in vogue in this world—rather, He is detested by it. Our God might be beautiful to those of us who know Him, but we must realize He isn't beautiful to those in rebellion against His rule and reign.

Psalm 2:2,4 states, "The kings of the earth set themselves, and the rulers take counsel together, against the LORD, and against His anointed, saying...He that sitteth in the heavens shall laugh: the LORD shall have them in derision."

God does not cry out, "Please like Me!" He doesn't offer the world's kings and rulers gifts to try to win their vote. He doesn't bribe them with beer and brat barbecues on the church's front lawn. No. The Bible says, "He that sits in the heavens shall laugh" and "the LORD shall have them in derision."

The bravehearted path is not about comfort and ease, but a kingdom and a glory. It is not about capitulation, but stalwart conviction. It's about currying our King's good favor while fully recognizing the fact that the world will hate us as a result.

The Bible reminds us that to be friends with the world is to be an enemy of God.[7]

We would do well to remember that to be friends with God is to be an enemy of the world.

May we choose our friends wisely.

Enough of this cool Christianity—let's get back to following Christ!

Part Four

MIND WIDE OPEN

Standing for nothing, falling for everything

Thirteen

EMERGING with the TRUTH INTACT

It is quite possible that the number one question I am asked these days is, "Eric, what are your thoughts on the emergent church movement?"

Those who know my conservative bent and my leanings toward the historic roots of the faith fully expect me to provide them a juicy rant about how heretical the whole movement is. But, whereas the emergent movement is out in la-la land in most of their doctrinal notions, they *are* on to something. And it is something that I too feel is true, important, and at the very center of what God is doing in the world.

Make no mistake: Just because I believe that the church should stand *contra mundum* and defend the truth against all comers does not mean that I think that everything that calls itself the church or truth or Christian should be blindly and unquestioningly defended.

You see, I truly believe that we are on the cusp of another reformation. Or, I should say, *we better be* on the cusp of another reformation. We are at a tipping point. And I actually agree with the emergent movement on the fact that the church, in its current state, is outdated, outmoded, and out-to-lunch. And basically the prognosis is, "Emerge and live, or stagnate and die."

Which church would you rather be a part of? The emergent or the stagnant? The answer is obvious. That's why the emergent church is a movement. *They are going somewhere.* And many of the people who are marching in step with this movement have joined up for no other reason than they are sick and tired of sitting around in church pews week after week doing nothing.

The main problem I have with this movement is that they are bludgeoning the name and nature of Jesus Christ into jelly while trying to "emerge." They aren't emerging like Athanasius, but like Arius. They aren't reforming like Luther, but are like Pope Leo with his novel theological inventions. They have the right idea about what is wrong but they are missing one very important piece of equipment for determining what is right—*the love of the truth* (which has a lot to do with the fact that they actually don't believe there is one definable truth).

The bestselling books in Christendom today are emergent. These guys are smart. You would almost think they sit around all day long and study the disenfranchised American churchgoer and then design a religion to fit precisely with what that massive demographic is looking for.

That's not exactly how I like to spend my time; so I was kind of surprised when I was asked the other day if I would consider writing an emergent book. I thought to myself, *How ironic is that? Emergent,* which literally means "to come out of," has so many other connotations these days. It means "conversational style, young thinking, crass, vulgar and hip," and "philosophically progressive." I honestly don't know if I truly fall into the framework of any of the above-mentioned categories. I am young, but I don't know if I'm young thinking. I am philosophically different than the modern Christian system, but I would deem myself philosophically old-fashioned rather than philosophically progressive. I'm emergent, yes, but emergent in a completely different way.

I believe that there is an entire army of Christians who fall into my same position. They live in a postmodern world, but they are not postmodern devotees. They're not satisfied with the status quo and are wanting to see reformation, but they want reformation with the historic moorings of the church triumphantly intact. They are what I call *historic emergent.* They want to emerge out of dry, dead religion, but not into some milquetoast, quasi-Christianity that passes around hugs and kisses and then concludes the meeting by saying, "Save the trees, save the whales, recycle your plastics, and therefore, prove yourself to be a follower of Jesus."[1] This army of Christians, though not always the most vocal, believes ardently that there is an absolute truth and that His name is Jesus Christ, and they desperately want this King of all kings to be seen, known, and trumpeted to the nations.

So I've been thinking. Maybe we should reclaim the word *emergent.* After all, it's a great word. It's loaded with meaning. It's just currently held hostage by a band of mushy-minded believers who have the right idea but the wrong method.

So, if we were to take back the word *emergent* and define it to mean "those hungry for the fullest measure of God, the deepest depths of devotion, the highest heights of maturity, the purest understanding of Scripture, the holiest pattern for living, the hottest flame of fire kindled upon the human soul, and the brightest light of Christ emanating through the life given over and wholly abandoned to the love and grace of our King," then maybe I *could* write an emergent book. And maybe you, too, if you are anything like me, might consider becoming an emergent Christian.[2]

This particular section of the book is a bit longer than all the others. And that is because this section is at the center of the fray. When the manly stuff is removed, all sorts of interesting things begin to creep into the pulpits of the church.

Fourteen

STRETCHING THE TRUTH

Rob Bell, the pastor of Mars Hill Church in Grand Rapids, Michigan, is one of the most likeable guys around. He's a great communicator, with a story for every situation and a great knack for the artistic. You can't spend five minutes with this guy without a smile cracking all over your face. I have many dear friends who absolutely love him. But when I started praying and asking God to infuse a little more Luther into my bloodstream, I immediately found that guys like Rob Bell get under my skin quicker than anyone else. Why? Because he reminds me of me.

Isn't that the way it always is? We have a tendency to be disturbed more by things that closely resemble our greatest weaknesses than by things that we can't relate to at all. Rob Bell is a lot like Erasmus (see pages 102-09). And, I'm sorry to say, he gives evidence of being more interested in attracting his audiences with beauty and allure than in representing the unchanging, undiluted truth of the gospel. And I can definitely relate to such a tug and pull within my own life. I have a strange attraction toward the applause of the crowd, and yet at the same time I really want to be pleasing to God. But when I aim for both, inevitably I end up kowtowing to the crowd, and God's truth ends up suffering.

Pastor Bell is a fantastic and very convincing writer, but he is also a self-acknowledged "truth stretcher." Uh-oh. That doesn't sound very good now, does it? No, he's not an outright liar. It's just that in his book, *Velvet Elvis,* he likens truth to the springs on a trampoline—these springs stretch up, down, and all around depending upon who happens to be jumping on the trampoline. To Pastor Bell, truth is *supposed* to be "stretched"—after all, according to him, that is the very essence of its "springy" nature.[1] Truth, according to our friend Rob, conforms to culture and to an individual's needs, and it seems to do all sorts of wild gymnastic-like twists and turns when coming out of his mouth or his pen.

Since Pastor Bell is making statements that make me squirm, let me make a statement that would certainly make him squirm. *Truth does not stretch. It does not adapt. It does not placate.* The Word of God is unchanging and does not shift in its meaning from generation to generation. Oh, we might want it to, but, like God, it is the same yesterday, today, and forever. I know, I know, I sound like some raving fundamentalist with wire-rimmed glasses waving around a 55-pound Bible. But even at risk of being lumped in with all those dour-faced modernists, I'm going to draw a line in the sand and say, "Here I stand!"

Now, I know exactly what Rob would say to that last statement. He would say, "Eric, you're living in Brickworld." *Brickworld,* according to Rob, is an imaginary place, a place invented by religious people where truth, facts, and doctrines are laughably thought to be constructed of solid bricks instead of stretchy springs. In his book *Velvet Elvis,* Rob sneeringly refers to this literalistic interpretation of the Bible as "Brickianity."[2]

So I live in Brickworld, huh? I'm really not sure I can take that as an insult. You see, bricks and rocks have a lot in common. And even though I don't see anything about trampolines or springs in Scripture, I do see a lot about rocks.

There is a specific rock up in Estes Park, Colorado, that Leslie and I are particularly fond of. It's right at the apex of a gorgeous hike around Lily Lake, and the view there is spectacular. Over the years we have stood on that rock numerous times and taken quite a few pictures. It's amazing, but over the past decade that rock hasn't changed a bit. In fact, I'm guessing that rock hasn't changed shape over multiple thousands of years. You see, rocks don't adjust to each new generation of hikers; rather, each new generation of hikers is forced to adjust to them. And much to the chagrin of many like Pastor Bell, Jesus is a rock. His truth is a rock, and when we build on this rock then we are stabilized through wind, rains, and all manner of harsh weather.[3] As a rock, God isn't changing to meet the times, He isn't stretching in order to be more inviting, more pleasant, or more presentable. He is the Great I AM, the Chief Cornerstone, the same yesterday today and forever.[4]

Pastor Bell is on the front lines of a movement that has brought and is bringing the idea of "flexible truth" to the mainstream modern church. Now, I realize that flexible truth sounds like an oxymoron, and that's because it is. But this concept seems to make perfect sense to those of the trampoline mentality.

"I just don't buy into a lot of this Christian stuff!" I've heard quite a few young collegiates proclaim in the past few years.

"What do you mean by Christian stuff?" I ask, very interested.

"You know, the Bible being all perfect, Jesus being the only way, Christianity being the only recipe—you know, stuff like that."

"But you still call yourself a Christian?" I ask, quite perplexed.

"Yeah. But I'm not a Christian like that old fundamentalist regime!"

"How's that?"

"Well for starters, I don't think it's my job to shove truth down people's throats!"

"I see."

"And I just think that a lot of other religions have a lot of great things to say, too."

"Really?"

"Yeah! You see, I was reading this book the other day that was talking about how truth wasn't all stiff and rigid, but flexible—more like the springs on a trampoline. And the idea rang so true! But so many Christians get it wrong. They treat truth as if it were a brick wall. But I just feel that truth should be more of an experience than a formula."

Anyway, you get the point. It's a Christianity that isn't even Christianity. Why they continue to label what they're professing as "Christian" is what mystifies me. Christianity is being morphed into something quite strange and unfamiliar right before our very eyes. Everyone is so tired of hypocritical Bible-thumpers that we are swinging instead into this camp of mushy-minded Bible-discarders.

Nowadays, truth has a very unique adversary, and this adversary is sort of like a slimy slug. It's hard to pick up, and it has no vertebrae to help define its shape. In other words, it's "springy." I hear the statement all the time from serious-minded Christians attempting to live scripturally sound lives for Christ, "I sense that something is wrong with what this guy is saying, but I just can't put my finger on it." And then there's the other famous quote I've heard: "It's like trying to nail Jell-O to the wall!"

The manly stuff is not ashamed of being defined. It will boldly proclaim, "Here I stand!" When truth is made of rock, it forces people to be more concrete in their relation to it. But when it loses its solidity, suddenly everything becomes vague and theoretical. And when truth is vague and theoretical, it can look like anything you want it to look like. It can mean whatever you personally think it should mean. And it is precisely at this point that it ceases to be truth at all.

This is known as postmodernism—or what I term the open mind.

And even though many emergent Christians are applauding our migration toward the enshrining of the open mind (aka *postmodernism*) as the new cardinal virtue of the church, I will readily admit *I am not one of them*. My main reason for such a dissent has to do with the way it makes truth mushy. And mushy truth creates a paralysis of action in the human life.

You'll realize once you get around to reading "The Canon-mind" beginning on page 183 that while I am wholeheartedly opposed to the open-mind mentality, I by no means am against the idea of having an open mind toward truth, to the voice of God, or the radical ideas of the kingdom of Christ. The problem with the open mind is that it isn't just open to God, but it is open to every other voice as well. When we submit ourselves to Christ to be transformed by the renewing of our minds, the result is not open-mindedness (as would commonly be practiced today), close-mindedness, or even narrow-mindedness, but rather, it is what could be termed *canon-mindedness*. And canon-mindedness is something to behold!

Fifteen

THE PARALYSIS OF INFINITY

I must forewarn you: This chapter is a bit more intellectually weighty than the others. It's critical stuff, but it's the kind of stuff that, if administered in too high a dosage, can result in smoke coming out of the ears. If that inclines you to skip the chapter, I would encourage instead that you give it a whirl and not be shy. You might be surprised and really enjoy it. In fact, I fully expect that you will.

———

In ancient times, there were those who believed the Earth to be flat and those who believed the Earth to be round. The flats probably didn't venture very far from the shoreline for fear that they may be approaching that fateful Edge of the earth. But the rounds, not bound by crazy superstitions, were moved by truth, and as a result discovered an entirely new world.

If this debate were still going on today, the open-mind camp would probably feel that the wisest course of action is to not take sides on the issue at all, for surely it would be intellectually arrogant to claim to know which group was right and which was wrong. I mean, after all, great men have been debating this issue for thousands of years, and who are we, they would say, to pass judgment on such a profound subject as this?

But don't be fooled by the pseudohumility. This is really just another way of saying that the truth can't be known. Which, of course, is in and of itself patently untrue. But if you believe it to be true, even though your belief does not alter reality, it does completely alter the way you interact with the reality.

Let me explain.

Let's say that the open-mind group takes up a position (if you can call it that) that both theories (the flat and the round) have merit, but that neither is right or wrong. Aren't they then in the best position to act on either theory? Well, actually, if you have an open mind about the shape of the earth and choose not to side with either the flats or the rounds, you, by default, in the real world, would end up behaving as a flat.

You see, the only people who are actually going to behave as rounds—getting into ships and setting sail for the distant horizon—are those who are absolutely committed to the point of staking their life on the belief that the earth *is* round and that they are sailing, not to their doom, but to the discovery of new and distant lands.

All of the rest, however, whether confirmed flats or noncommitted open minds, will behave the same. What kind of idiot flat would get onto a ship sailing for the edge of the world and what undecided open mind would book passage aboard a ship headed for a destination that he refuses to even acknowledge the existence of?

In other words, the only way to get to somewhere is to commit *to* something. Those who will commit to nothing stay exactly where they are.

Now, what if news begins to spread that a new world has been discovered on the far side of the Atlantic—a world full of gold, beauty, and lots of real estate for the taking? The flats would claim it a lie intended to coax them off the end of the Earth. The rounds would excitedly begin to build boats, each launching their own grand adventure. But the open minds would be paralyzed. By keeping all their options open in regard to what may or may not be true, they have supplied themselves with an infinite number of options, probabilities, and possible realities. The problem is, open-minders have a hard time settling on any *one* option as the "correct" option because that would require a judgment which would, of course, mean that the other options were "wrong," and this the open mind cannot abide. Open-minders, therefore, often end up imprisoned by their own inability to decide on a clear course of action based upon the facts because they are constantly questioning the reality of the facts themselves.

I call this the paralysis of infinity—infinite options, but no ability to choose, define, or decide on any single one as correct.

As Shakespeare once said, "That way madness lies."[1]

Think about this: The reluctance to acknowledge truth to be true or facts to be factual in no way alters the truth or the facts. But it does completely alter the way *you* interact with them, and therefore, the way you live your life.

Among those who discovered the New World there were no fence-sitters. Each and every one of them had reached a decision and tendered an answer to the great question of their time: Is the earth flat, or is it round? They had each picked a side and staked a claim. And their decision led them to conclusions that led them to accept certain courses of action, such as building ships and setting sail, as valid, and to reject others, such as sitting around for another 200 years debating the issue to death as unreasonable.

Their decision led to beliefs, their beliefs led to actions, and the rest, as they say, is history.

And what of those open minds of the time who refused to weigh in on this great question? What of those who refused to make what they called "arrogant and foolish assumptions about things that could not possibly be known"? What of them? What did *they* accomplish? What did *they* contribute to society at large? History's only remembrance of them is to acknowledge that there were at that time some dissenters.

Those who abstained from the fray of decision became nothing more than a byword—a footnote to the history and deeds of men who dared to decide.

We should always remember—and never forget—that those who will commit to nothing, who stand for nothing, and who risk for nothing, in the end, rarely accomplish anything.

Life is all about decisions. And every decision in favor of one thing is a decision against something else. In a strange way, freedom is found in removing options and clarifying focus, not by hoarding possibilities and embracing obscurity. The flats, even though wrong in their opinion of reality, are probably a happier bunch than the open minds simply because they at least have a defined worldview. They aren't going anywhere, but at least they know why they aren't going anywhere. Meanwhile, the open minds sit self-conflicted in a boat somewhere near the shores of Palos de la Frontera,[2] wondering if they should stay or go.

Let's take a look at how this indecisive, inconclusive open mind has crept into the modern church:

On Monday:

Tony, a young man attending the local college here in Fort Collins, Colorado, reads a popular Christian book that presents ideas that are wholly incompatible with Scripture and leads to a very self-centered rendition of Christianity.

Then on Tuesday:

Tony attends a conference at which Joe Gospel-truth is speaking. He hears a message that is grounded in Scripture and promotes a Christ-centered rendition of Christianity (which I may contend is the *only* version of Christianity espoused in Scripture). Tony is deeply impacted by the power of the gospel as presented in Joe Gospel-truth's message, and he embraces it as true and right as he weeps on his knees before God.

On Wednesday:

I discover in conversation with Tony that the erroneous message he heard on Monday somehow still remains lodged in his thinking, and that the message on Tuesday has now been *added* to Tony's trophy case of "options."

The open mind, wanting to keep all of its options open, accepts everything and rejects nothing. Somehow this mind-set allows for two opposing thoughts, or systems of belief, to coexist within the same worldview. In the good old days, it used to be that accepting the truth required men to make a decision about reality that automatically kicked out the error in their heads and their hearts. It used to be that if you had truly come to believe that the Earth was round, this booted out the notion that the Earth could somehow still be flat. Likewise, if you accepted the truth about Christ and His claims, it removed the error about Buddha as a means of salvation. But the open-minder can hear the truth of Scripture and somehow hold it loosely enough that it never eradicates all the other opposing worldviews that are contending for Christ's rightful throne within the mind.

Yet the biblical worldview is one of replacement.

We are taken out of darkness and into light, out of death into life, from the mind of the world to the mind of Christ, from the image of Adam to the image of Jesus—it is always a transition *out of* one thing and *into* another. It is never an addition of one thing *to* another. The Bible is all about purity of ingredients, *not* mixture of ingredients.

What fellowship hath righteousness with unrighteousness? and what communion hath light with darkness? And what concord hath Christ with Belial? or what part hath he that believeth with an infidel? And what agreement hath the temple of God with idols?...Wherefore come out from among them, and be ye separate, saith the Lord, and touch not the unclean thing; and I will receive you.[3]

The biblical worldview is one of displacement.

There is absolutely no precedent for "mixture" in the Christian life—only the displacement of one thing by the arrival of another. Light arrives, darkness flees; truth arrives, lies evaporate; life arrives, death goes bye-bye.

The biblical worldview isn't springy. Both replacement and displacement require *one* option to be chosen as the correct option, and this requires a judgment to be made—which would, of course, mean that the other options are wrong. The round-earth theory is accepted and the flat-earth theory rejected. Truth is embraced, and lies are refuted. Light is chosen, and darkness is expelled. The truth that grabbed hold of Tony on Tuesday yearns to violently put to death the cancerous error that had begun to infect his mind on Monday, so that on Wednesday Tony can move forward and chart a clear course to the New World.

"Come on, Eric!" I can hear someone say. "So what! At least this Tony guy found the truth!"

Yes, Tony may have heard the truth on Tuesday and appraised it as correct, but as long as the error from Monday still remains lodged inside his soul come Wednesday, it will fight against the truth, canceling out its effects for the remainder of that week and every week that follows. It's like a brain with a tumor lodged in its frontal lobe: Sure it's still a functioning brain for the time being, but the tumor *will* eventually cause it to cease to function. If the tumor isn't removed, then it will ultimately make the brain completely inoperative. And in the same way, if the truth does not displace the lie, then the lie *will* displace the truth. These elements are at war one with the other, and it is imperative that exclusive acceptance be shown toward one and intolerance to the other.

We must decide. We must choose.

"But wouldn't it be intellectually arrogant to claim to know definitively what is right and what is wrong? I mean, after all, great men have been debating this issue for thousands of years, and who are we to pass judgment on such a profound subject as this?"

That statement sounds good, but it is really just a throwing up of the hands at any attempt to know the truth in any fashion, shape, or form.

I believe that the open mind is a way of thinking and living that is a result of the abandonment of the manly side of truth—the side of truth that contends and wrestles, that debates and confronts, that stands and, having done all, stands some more. But the open mind is a surrender, a quitting, a laying down of the sword, a weariness in well doing, a retreat from the battle for the faith once and for all delivered to the saints. The open mind, for lack of a more politically correct way of saying it, is a purely emasculated manner of thinking that is unwilling to wage war against error. It fights for nothing, stands for nothing, never shoots the horse, is all-accepting, tolerant of lies, and embracing of contradiction. In the name of love, acceptance, and unity, it never requires someone to pick a side.

I'm labeling the open mind as an emasculated pattern for thinking and relating to life, and I'm sure that will get me into a bit of hot water with some of my readership. However, the open mind is a swing from a very unhealthy, masculine, left-brained pattern for thinking and relating to life known commonly as modernism. (*Modernism* is nothing more than the worship of logic, rationale, and reason to the exclusion of relationship, experience, and intuition). The open mind (aka *postmodernism*) is an evidence on an out-of-balance feminine emphasis on feeling and intuition in our society and in the church. It is very existential. I'm sorry to use such an intimidating word, but let me explain. *Existential* essentially means that it is highly subjective and based on feelings, not on facts. Right and wrong, to an open mind, are determined by how someone personally feels toward certain truths. If he resonates with the idea and it makes him feel healthy and whole, then "it's truth." But if he is repulsed by the idea and it makes him feel guilty and needful, then "it's false."

This is exactly how the open mind can allow so many contradictory "truths" about reality to coexist in a single worldview. Without the manly emphasis on the accuracy of truth and the preservation of sound doctrine, as well as a willingness to wage war against error, the error remains cobbled together with the truth. The random, mismatched, and unlikely pieces are allowed into the puzzle *not* because they fit together, but because they all just "feel" like they belong together.

This type of reasoning may feel good, but it simply does not work. If you practiced open-mind mathematics, it wouldn't take long before you ran into difficulties. For instance, you might not like the outcome of the equation two plus two equals four, but your subjective feelings about the outcome mean nothing in the realm of reality. The long and short of it is that two plus two equals four whether you like it or not.

"Boy, this mathematics stuff just doesn't seem very springy; it seems more like brickmatics if you ask me."

"Where do these guys get off telling kids that two plus two has to equal four? That's so brickworld."

"No wonder kids are dropping out of school! And who can blame them, really? Now, if math and school in general could be more like a trampoline, where people could just come and jump without having to worry about a bunch of rules like two plus two equals four and stuff, then I bet a lot more kids would stick around. Of course, they wouldn't be learning to read, write, or do arithmetic but hey, that's all just details anyway. We shouldn't let hyperpractical, brickworld objections keep our children from experiencing a great education—or whatever it is you want to call it."

It's obvious that the open mind just has no place in a field like mathematics. In fact, every science would quickly turn into a gigantic mess if you introduced the open mind into it. I mean, would you rather fly in an airplane engineered and crafted after the intolerant laws of aerodynamics, or by an open-minder trying out his personal theories regarding flight?

Modernism, on the other hand, when it was in vogue this past century, was very intellectual, fact-based, and often cold and unfeeling. Truth was oft-treated as distant and pre-defined and therefore heartless and uncaring. Many people, however, are rebelling against the straitjacket of modernism only to swing over into the equally serious and opposite error of the open mind.

But, according to the Bible, truth is neither a feeling nor some distant and detached idea; truth is a person—a person known as Jesus Christ, who wasn't distant but came and dwelt among us.[4] He wasn't predictable, but He was shockingly lavish in His sense for the dramatic. He wasn't heartless and uncaring, but in fact He gave up His life in order to bring us into an intimate acquaintance with Himself.

Modernism's strength was that it gave accurate definitions of truth, but its weakness was that it often failed to deliver the living substance of truth. For all its logic, scriptural intelligence, and concise catechisms, modernism failed. It basically inspired a religion that was stuck in the head and disconnected from the heart. It could define love, joy, peace, and victory, but it couldn't impart them to an audience. It tried to reason its way into Heaven rather than yield its way.

Plain and simple, modernism didn't work in large part due to the fact that it lacked the feminine side of truth—the side that seeks real relationship, genuine community, and authentic heart-to-heart encounters.

And if I may be so bold, I am confident that this new experiment of open-mindedness will also fail the church simply because it is an unhealthy pendulum swing that excludes the contributions of the manly stuff into the body of Christ the same way that modernism often excluded compassion, beauty, relationship, and the value of experience.

I will readily admit that the advocates of the open mind and the emergent church are doing some things right. They are seeking real relationships, genuine community, and authentic heart-to-heart encounters, but now the church is missing the accurate definitions of truth and the necessary love-based intolerance that must come when truth is defined and understood. The pendulum has swung too far to the left.

For most of our lives, my entire generation has been spoon-fed "emasculated mentalities." We were raised to be tolerant, and therefore we have become tolerant even intellectually with what we allow into our belief system. We are tolerant to the point that our open-mindedness not only allows ideas that conflict with each other to remain side by side, but also ideas that are in conflict with the Word of God. We hug the error in our life instead of showing prejudice against it. We are dangerously inclusive in our Christianity and in our doctrine rather than realizing that the only way the gospel works is if it displaces and replaces everything in our hearts, minds, and bodies that stands against the image of Christ being born in us.

The Bible puts it like this: "Casting down imaginations, and every high thing that exalteth itself against the knowledge of God, and bringing into captivity every thought to the obedience of Christ."[5] Do we want the image of Christ to rise within us? Then the impostors must be "cast down." There will be no sharing of our soul's throne, only abdication, for our God has said that He will share His glory with no man. Remember: God's method is displacement and replacement, never addition.

Tolerance and open-mindedness have become the cardinal virtues of our society. But like science, it is not open-mindedness, unconditional acceptance, or tolerance that is Christianity's main objective—it is simply the truth.

At the heart of the gospel is an intolerance for sin, an intolerance for the flesh, and an intolerance for selfishness—just as in aerodynamics there is an intolerance for the idea of airplanes made of cement. If reality dictates that cement is a material inhospitable to flight, then we build our planes out of aluminum. You might be surprised, but aerodynamic engineers are an overwhelmingly prejudiced bunch—prejudiced against cement, that is (lead isn't terribly popular, either). Yes, I know it appears to be a narrow-minded position, but it is by no means an ignorant one. Nothing personal against cement, but it just doesn't work.

For truth to thrive and for flight to be achieved, the cement in our plane factories has to be replaced with aluminum. Otherwise our planes will never get off the ground. And in this age of the mushy open mind, the error in our heads, hearts, and churches has to be kicked out by the truth or we will not survive another generation as a significant force for good in the Western world.

The sad thing is that the error isn't getting kicked out because, like Tony, we have become infected by the open mind. We don't want to have to choose to stand for certain things and reject others. We want to somehow find a way to embrace everything and everyone without having to oppose anything.

It would seem that we've all become too religiously correct to dare to confront the error in our midst. We've grown weary of contending for the faith. We just don't want to think about it anymore. We have become so afraid of being labeled intolerant, judgmental, legalistic, fundamental, and elitist in regard to our beliefs that we have quietly turned down the volume on what we have to say, assuming that we have anything to say in the first place. And so we stay wishy-washy and nonconfrontational. Until finally, after a while, we find ourselves deciding that it's probably for the best that we not take sides on these issues at all, for it would certainly be intellectually arrogant to claim to know which group is right and which is wrong. I mean, after all (and here I insert the modern mantra one last time), great men have been debating these issues for thousands of years, and who are we to pass judgment on such profound subjects as those that the church and the world now face?

And so we waste our lives away sitting in a boat somewhere near the shores of Palos de la Frontera, wondering if we should stay or go.

Sixteen

WISHFUL THINKING
IS NO THINKING AT ALL

You and I are responsible.

We are responsible for deciding what we believe, and then to live accordingly.

We are responsible for choosing whom we will serve, and then to yield.

We are responsible for choosing between good and evil in thousands of areas of life.

That we must choose has already been decided. But the choosing itself has been left up to us. And what we choose will decide our fate.

The truth was entrusted to the body of Christ as a whole, and not just to its ministers. Each of us will be held accountable for knowing Scripture and, like the Bereans, testing everything we hear against it.[1] We can't rely upon our leaders to take us by the hand and point out to us everything that must be avoided. We must become the watchdog of our soul, of our homes, of our marriages, and of our churches.

There is something intrinsically woven into the fabric of the manly stuff that begs for something to defend, to protect, to guard. Traditionally it has been those who were "in touch" with their masculine side who have stood up to defend both hearth and home from those who would plunder and invade that sanctuary for their own gain. And this vanguard of defenders is not an exclusive men's club, it is also filled with the names of thousands of valiant women. Woe to the man who enters into a mother's lair to do harm to her cubs; regardless of size, he will be lucky to escape with his eyes intact.

But lately the manly stuff seems to be missing from the church. Where is the scrutinizing security guard standing watch at the vault of our mind, ensuring that nothing is amiss? Where is the ever-searching eye of the warrior as he stands atop the wall, scanning the horizon for any sign of the enemy of our soul?

Where has this vigilant attitude disappeared to? Have we forgotten that Satan, our arch-nemesis, stalks about day and night seeking those whom he may devour? Did he retire?

We have let down our guard.

"Don't be so uptight," people say. "You're majoring on the minors. Just relax a bit!"

And while the watchmen sleep, the enemy has crept in.

Satan's invasion of the church hasn't been an all-out assault. You see, he doesn't want to awaken us from our pleasant dreams of peace and safety. Instead, he quietly and carefully tiptoes about his covert operations, sending his agents of silent death into our hearts, homes, and minds through a myriad unguarded avenues.

A perverted TV show here, a questionable movie there, a little racy language smattered into a conversation just to "keep it real." A few compromises on our belief about the absolute truth of Scripture. A few sins indulged. A few indiscretions overlooked. And all of a sudden, the enemy isn't at the gate—he's at the dining room table, he's sleeping in our bed, he's talking through our mouth, pawing through our mind, and living in our skin.

We have an enemy.

We need guardians.

We need women and men young and old alike to get a healthy dose of the manly stuff infused back into their bloodstream and send the jackals that are ravaging the vineyard of Christ packing!

There is an unspoken urban legend that has been haunting the halls of the church. The Christian community seems to be under the disarming impression that there is some sort of vigilant watchdog group somewhere in the corridors of the Christian faith made up of a roomful of gray-haired Gandalf-types. This group scrupulously screens every book, every video, and every last candy wrapper headed for the shelves of Christian bookstores, standing guard, making sure that nothing of the enemy ever bears the name *Christian*. There is a naïve and innocent confidence that if it is labeled *Christian* that the label must be accurate. After all, it must have already been tested by those gray-haired watchdogs who scrutinized it carefully and sniffed every corner of it with their Spirit-sensitized noses.

Unfortunately, this is simply not true.

No one else is doing our job for us.

If someone told you that an elixir of three cups of sugar and five bars of chocolate melted down into a sauce and blended with a carton of vanilla ice cream was actually a cure for every human ailment, the idea may resonate with you rather quickly; it may even "feel" right. But that wouldn't mean that what he told you was actually correct.

It is not hard to give a message that sounds good but leads to an upset stomach, clogged arteries, or worse, a spiritually dead existence. All you have to do is make sure you give your audience exactly what they are wanting to hear, and they will grab hold of it with all the tenacity of a bulldog chomping a rubber chew toy.

For instance, tell a child that the world revolves around her, and you won't hear her complain even the slightest about your incorrect guidance. Tell a teenager that premarital sex and alcohol are important ingredients in the preparation of his leadership and social skills, and a large, understanding smile will fill his face as you speak your gnarled and twisted counsel. Tell an adult that there is nothing more to Christianity than being comfortable, happy, secure, self-gratified, and enfolded in the loving embrace of Abba, and churches will be filled to capacity once again!

What I'm trying to say is that you can't believe everything you hear or read, even if you did hear it on Christian radio or if it came from a Christian bookstore.

The Bible says that there are some who will come as a wolf in sheep's clothing.[2] Now if a wolf gets dressed up in a sheep outfit, it's probably a pretty good bet that he's not headed for the wolf lair but for the sheep pen. Satan is headed for a pulpit near you. He has impregnated Christian bookstores with wolfish products that parade as sheep but bring about nothing but destruction when consumed. Beware.

When the church sets aside the scrutinizing gaze of its watchmen—that masculine emphasis on defense and protection—as if it were unloving, then the body quickly loses its vigilance and ends up allowing packs of ravenous wolves, like Jane's son, into the sheep pen. Sure, an exclusively feminine church is a more inviting church. But who in the world benefits from being invited into a place packed with hungry wolves?

Seventeen

JUST BE REAL

When the open mind is allowed to run wild and unrestrained, truth loses its definition.

When truth loses its definition, we lose all perspective on what truth is even supposed to look like lived out in the real world.

And when we forget what truth looks like, we have no other standard to look to but ourselves. And we rarely rise higher than that standard.

———

There is a grassroots move toward openness and honesty within the body of Christ today. For years we covered up our sinful vices (obviously an unhealthy form of hypocrisy), but now we are wearing them like emblems of honor about our necks. I term it the "just be real" movement. It works like this:

"Just admit it, Brian—you masturbate. I know you do, because every guy does. It's all right to admit it, because admitting it is the first step towards God and peace with yourself."

Brian squirms. He is not used to being involved in a conversation in which such awkward things are discussed, let alone being asked to participate in the conversation.

After hearing a few other Christian guys confess to their addictions to pornography and their near-nightly practice of masturbation, Brian finally breaks down and confesses his own battles within that arena.

"I've never felt so free!" Brian acknowledges later. "I've been bound up in shame for the past ten years and now it's all out on the table. It feels so good to *just be real*."

The thrill of being real is something that, if you personally have never experienced it, is quite a wonderful thing. I, for one, love being real. In fact, it is my prayer that my every moment in every day would be governed by a true, authentic, and genuine behavior that springs forth from my life shared with God. My dream life would be a life without even a spot of fake in it. As Brian says, "It feels so good to *just be real.*"

But there is a problem with our modern Christian rendition of realness.

Historically in the church, being real was an initiation into the radical school of Christ. It was an abandonment of the false life that stood in the way of growth with Christ and an acknowledgment that everything about me is fake and weak, while everything about Christ is true and powerful. Being real simply meant, "I'm wrong, Christ is right!"

But today, being real is an initiation into the ranks of the cool brotherhood.

"We are all a mess, Brian, and now you are a self-acknowledged member of our gang. Welcome to the party!"

Being real today means acknowledging how "unlike Christ we really are down deep." And then, for some inexplicable reason, it stops there. And it's sad, but it seems the more unlike Christ you can prove that you are during your "real" confession, the more hip, the more attractive you are to the cool brotherhood.

We have become our own standard, and the standard is messy. We aspire to nothing higher than what we currently are. And the only hypocrisy is to not be true to ourselves.

In fact, hypocrisy no longer means "professing one thing while living another." It now means "professing one thing while not 'being real' about living another." The "bad, faker" Christians, we are told, fall into the first category, while the "good, honest" Christians are found in the second.

Whatever happened to the definition of a "good, honest" Christian as being someone who professes to follow Christ with his lips and then *actually* goes out and faithfully follows Him, day in and day out, with all his heart, mind, soul, and strength?

Do you want to know what happened to that definition? It has been discarded. It's been tossed aside, mostly because the vast majority of people don't even believe that such a creature exists. The truth is, many people would roll their eyes at the description in the paragraph above. "Come on, Eric," they say, "you need to get real. People who fit that profile are just selling you a bill of goods. If you could take just one peek for one second into their real life, you would see that they are just as dirty and sinful as everyone else."

The problem is, we no longer believe in a good, honest Christian who simply, faithfully, and consistently follows Jesus Christ day in and day out. In fact, in our heart of hearts, though we may never say it, we think that this breed of people are big liars.

Oddly enough, the only people whom we trust any more in Christianity—the only people whom we consider to be real, honest Christians—are those who come right out and testify not of the power of Christ transforming their lives, but of their own sinful indulgences, lusts, and indiscretions, and their complete inability to cease from a single one.

These are the new heroes of the emasculated, metrotheistic, emergent church. We don't revere those men and women who have become more than conquerors[1] through Jesus Christ and who beckon us by their example to do the same. Rather, we glorify those who wallow in their self-indulgent slavery to the flesh and thereby comfort us in our own.

It's sad, but being sinful, messy, and tainted in your Christianity has actually become a necessary requirement in order to have an influence within a large sector of the Christian world today. It's considered real, honest, and authentic, and let me tell you, *it's magnetic!* If you know your stuff in Christian communications, then you know what Christian audiences love—they love "dirt" on the speaker. And the more dirt, as a speaker, that you can provide your audience, the more likeable, credible, and compelling you will be.

The late Mike Yaconelli, the founder of Youth Specialties, wrote a book entitled *Messy Spirituality.* In the opening moments of the book, Mike establishes the fact that he is part of the cool brotherhood. Mike is real, loaded with authenticity, and potently honest:

> My life is a mess. After forty-five years of trying to follow Jesus, I keep losing him in the crowded busyness of my life. I know Jesus is there, somewhere, but it's difficult to make him out in the haze of everyday life...I want to have more victories than defeats, yet here I am, almost sixty, and I fail on a regular basis. If I were to die today, I would be nervous about what people

would say at my funeral. I would be happy if they said things like "He was a nice guy" or "He was occasionally decent" or "Mike wasn't as bad as a lot of people." Unfortunately, eulogies are delivered by people who know the deceased. I know what the consensus would be. "Mike was a mess."[2]

While Mike was alive, he was wildly popular. Why? Because he was "real." He gave his audience all the dirt, and as a result, they gave him the loftiest platforms from which to speak. He is basically the founder of the modern Christian youth worker movement and he has greatly influenced the thinking of an entire generation of Christian youth pastors.

There are those within our own ranks who are working feverishly to push an agenda forward that, whether intentionally or not, is undermining the rock-solid foundations of the faith. The enemy need crash no battering rams against our walls if the city falls under its own weight. And we are doing a fairly good job shooting the power of the gospel in the foot all by ourselves.

We have lost our grand expectations of God and His gospel. When our leaders on every side admit to living lives that are, at best, messy, but then don't press on to have Christ deliver them from their mess, what signal does that send to the rest of us as to what we should really expect in our own lives?

It used to be that credibility, in Christianity, was gained through evidencing the transforming power of Jesus Christ within your life. It was supernatural love, overwhelming joy, indescribable peace, demonstrated power, a triumphant perspective, and a fortified lifestyle that used to grab the attentions of the crowds. It was Christ at work in you that proved the authenticity of your voice and message.

But we live in different times.

Now, it's your angst, cynicism, crudeness, admitted defeat, and authenticity about your life of selfish compulsion that curries the favor of the masses.

Can't you just feel me setting you up for another comment about how Christianity is missing the manly stuff? Without the manly emphasis to conquer, to fix, along with that gritty willingness to wage war on all that is seeking to destroy us both as individuals and as a body, Christianity has become one gigantic hug of sinful messes. We are enshrining sinners instead of calling them to repentance. We are applauding the honesty of sex-addict pastors rather than calling them to either proclaim the gospel with their lives or get out from behind that pulpit. We no longer are a people who evidence the transforming power, might, and grandeur of the God of the universe. Yes, we may be honest about our lust, but none of us are expectant to see the Great God Jehovah rescue us from our lust.

I would guess eight out of ten modern Christians don't even believe that God desires to showcase His transforming power, might, and grandeur in their lives and in this world. Most Christians today don't even believe something as simple as, "God will free you from your addictions!" Let alone something as huge as, "God can heal the lame, give sight to the blind, and make the deaf to hear again." In fact, it isn't cool in Christianity today to believe such bizarre things. It is considered intellectually inferior theology to actually think that God is desiring to do the same things today that He did when He launched this whole Christian thing in the first place. It is far more in style to proclaim from the highest mountaintop, "I'm a mess! So don't feel bad if you are, too!"

Can you imagine Jesus Christ saying, "Let's start this whole Christianity thing off with a bang and then, suddenly and without any warning, let's take all the muscle, the power, the triumph out of the whole machinery and leave these weakling Christians to sit around in the stew of their sin for the final few thousand years until I return"?

Okay, I'll just say it: Where is the manly stuff?!

Eighteen

FAITH OR FEAR—
CHOOSE YOUR MASTER

Faith was once a radical thing. Historically it has always been a chalk line with two opposing kingdoms standing on either side, and two kings proclaiming to the human soul, "Which side are you on? You are either with me or against me! There is no place on my side of the chalk line for halfhearted adherents!"

The idea of faith needs a fresh infusion of the manly stuff! Because without the manly stuff, faith has become some kind of "counseling session" between God and man.

God says, "So how are you doing today, Pete?"

Pete responds, "I'm okay, I guess. I've just got this whole anger issue flaring up again."

God says, "Oh, I'm sorry to hear that."

Pete responds, "Yeah. It's a real bummer. My wife left me and took the kids because of it. I lost my job at the factory because of it. And I'm on more than a few friends' blacklists thanks to it."

God says, "Well, just know I'm here for you if you ever want to talk about it."

Pete smiles and says, "Thanks, God! It's just good to know that You are there!"

Pete might know that God is there. Pete might know God listens to his prayers. Pete might even know that God isn't going to hold his anger problem over his head and say, "I've had enough of you, Pete, to Hell with you!" But Pete has nothing of the real substance of faith. Pete is hanging out on the enemy's side of the chalk line, staring at God's side and saying, "Yeah, I believe there's a God."

Pete most certainly does believe that there is a God. He even believes that God will save him from Hell in the next life. It's just that he fully expects to continue living in the Hell-on-earth he's currently in until the very day he dies. Pete doesn't believe in the power of his God to actually rescue him, change him, and radically alter his life in order to demonstrate to this world the glory of Jesus Christ!

But when you plant the manly stuff back into the construct of faith, it becomes something altogether different. It becomes powerful, majestic, and regenerative—a radical instrument of change within the human life and within this desperate world. It turns weakling Petes into heroic Peters.

Christianity is built on one very basic thing: faith. And without faith there isn't much left in the whole operation, because everything in Christianity that matters operates with it. If you want grace, you need faith. If you want to know God's love and live in God's love, again it's faith that provides the passport. Salvation? Yep, faith. Victory? Uh-huh, faith. Holiness? Faith. Righteousness? Faith.

Hebrews 11:6 says that "without *faith* it is impossible to please [God]." Then again in Galatians 5:6 we read that, the only thing that counts is *faith* expressing itself in love. Oh, and yet again in Ephesians 2:8, "By grace are ye saved through *faith*." It would appear that a lot rests on this idea of faith, and in fact, a lot does. In this whole gospel schematic, faith is the linchpin. If faith is absent, then the gospel is rendered powerless in a human life. Faith is the soul fuel upon which the gospel spark kindles and sets aflame.

We need a faith that isn't missing its masculine emphasis—a faith that actually fixes what is broken, that is willing to wage war for what is right, and that is determined to conquer by the power of God. This isn't a faith that embraces mountains but moves them. This isn't a faith that wilts in the heat of the battle but wrestles until God's deliverance is wrought in the Earth. It's a faith more like the Jacob variety,[1] the kind that says, "This is what God said He would do, and so I'm going to wrestle in prayer until it becomes a reality." It's a faith that includes the manly stuff and gives God no escape route—but rather, holds God to His Word and says, "You promised!"

Faith, with manly stuff intact, refuses to accept the fact that the natural world is not bearing evidence of God's claim on this Earth. It refuses to accept the notion that there is even such a thing as unanswered prayer. The concept is completely foreign; there is simply no such notion in God's economy.

Hudson Taylor's mother kneeled down one day when her son was 16 and said to God, "I will not rise until my son has seen the light." Not only was Hudson Taylor saved that day, but the world was forever changed through this one woman's demonstration of a fighting, prevailing faith—a faith that is willing to go to war for the son she loves and tirelessly wrestle for his soul.

Such a faith erupts with passion to remove the stigma of contradiction from being associated with the name of God. It thunders, "God said it, and it *will* be done—I'll stake my life on it!" Faith, in all its fullness, will persist, knock, beg, ask, and wrestle until the realities of the cross are fully evidenced in this natural world.

Why have we become a bunch of weak-willed nerfs? And why are we rolling over and accepting such defeat? Let's rise up with prayer and fasting and wrestle through the night until we lay hold of God and all that He has promised!

According to the Bible, faith is absolute, unwavering, all-out-confident, die-hard assurance, and die-to-prove-it certainty in the person of Jesus Christ and His Word. The long and short is that if God says He will do something, you can take it to the bank and place unreserved confidence in the fact that it *will* be done!

Faith is something that is best described in terms of battle. There needs to be a sense of danger about the idea of faith; otherwise the whole thing loses its zing and its sense of gravity. So imagine you are a soldier on the beaches of Normandy in World War II. You find yourself suddenly exposed to enemy fire. There is smoke, shrapnel, and general chaos all about. If you stay put, you are a dead man. Your commander shouts, "Charge to the cliffs! Now!" You are in a position of grave decision. Everything inside of you is wanting to jump in the water and try to hide from the bullets, or possibly see if you can find room next to that other man over there who is hiding behind a rock crying out for his mommy to save him. But your commander said, "Charge!" To obey such a command seems like insanity to your natural mind. To charge is to go head-on into the line of fire. But faith is abandonment to your commander's voice even at the expense of life and limb. Faith is trusting with a radical confidence that your commander sees more clearly than you do and that he knows what is best in this and every situation. And faith is also obedience, instant and decisive to whatever your superior officer requests.

Our Commander in Heaven has spoken, and He didn't stutter. And faith is the radical die-if-I-must adherence to His voice and to His every command. It's a forsaking of my natural reasoning as the means by which I will filter through and judge my life and decisions from this moment forward. If bullets are flying and my King shouts, "Charge! Now!" then there is no place for hesitation, for appealing to the natural voice of reason. My King said charge...I'm charging! It's an abandonment to God's thoughts, God's ways, God's agenda. God says, "I am asking for everything, for all your confidences to be placed in My ability to perform on your behalf."

Does this offend our natural mind? Absolutely!

That's why the very first action taken by faith, as the ruling principle within the human soul, is to hush the voice of doubt and to stick spiritual duct tape over its mouth. For doubt is the voice of the natural man—it is heavily biased towards self and its agenda, and is naturally antagonistic to the incoming regime of the Spirit of God.[2]

As dangerous and seemingly ignorant as this might seem to our natural minds, faith is wholly given to the opinion of God and trusts it implicitly. Faith is willing to forego the opinion of men and stake everything on the opinion of God. Faith has the gall to actually believe that God is who He says He is and that He is perfectly faithful to take care of His children when we simply entrust ourselves to Him. Such an act is not dangerous and ignorant, but perfectly in alignment with the way we were created.

Faith is fiercely loyal to the Word of God, and even at the risk of public ridicule, it is willing to put all its chips on God and live accordingly.

Does this look like idiocy to the world? Of course it does! But last time I checked, we aren't supposed to be concerned about what this world thinks of us. Isn't God's opinion the only one that really matters?

Nineteen

THE NEW ATHEIST AND THE MANLY STUFF

My buddy Ben tossed a magazine at me the other day while we were chatting at Starbucks. I quickly pooh-poohed any association with said magazine and shoved it back towards his side of the small table with a polite, "No thanks!"

Ben knows that I spend hardly a second of any given month reading secular journals, magazines, or commentaries that bash Christian ideas and mentalities. I really don't care what the world thinks about Christianity. I care far more about what Christianity thinks about Jesus Christ. That said, I did end up taking a peek, this past November, at the issue of *Wired* magazine that Ben was laboring hard to get me to read. He simply reshoved it back to my side of the table and with a raise of his eyebrows said, "Trust me! Just read it!"

A few days later I found an extra few minutes, fixed myself a hot mug of chai, picked up the article, and sat down to read. My mug of chai never got touched. I can definitely say, after reading this very disturbing rant against Christianity and the whole idea of faith, that I was freshly reminded why I don't fill my mind with that kind of garbage day in and day out. However, this was more than a mere rant—this was a call to arms against the "scourge" of Christianity. The article was entitled "The New Atheist," and to say it mildly, it was quite alarming.

The modern church, apparently, doesn't have the corner on emergent movements, because the atheists have started one of their own. It's strangely reminiscent of an old-timey revival. It's a heartfelt call for all the self-proclaimed atheists to place it all on the line for what they believe to be true. The problem is, what this group believes to be true is that faith in Jesus Christ is a hindrance to healthy society and a blockade from true social reform. Basically the message is, "If you truly believe that God is a myth, then stand up and, in the name of all that is reasonable, do something to stamp out this plague of religious faith!"

Gary Wolf, the man who wrote the article, made a statement that sent a chill up my spine:

"My Friends," he says to his readership (which obviously doesn't include me), "I must ask you an important question today: Where do you stand on God?...It is time to declare our positions...We are called upon, we lax agnostics, we noncommittal nonbelievers, we vague deists who would be embarrassed to defend antique absurdities like the Virgin Birth...or any other blatant myth; we are called out, we fence-sitters, and told to help exorcise this debilitating curse: the curse of faith."[1]

Here is the irony: The New Atheists are out to exorcise the demon of faith. But right inside our own churches there are wolves already laboring hard at the grindstone of doubt, whittling away the faith of believers down to a sliver so small that it hardly seems there at all. Gone are the days of the "good, honest" Christian who simply believed God and who then went on to base her entire existence on that belief, consistently following Jesus Christ day in and day out. True living faith has become passé in the corridors of the modern church—some even consider it a show of ignorance, a presumption upon God. We, as the church, have become literally skittish at the notion of being all-out-confident and convinced about what God defines as truth. We would rather remain "springy."

A man named Sam Harris, a neuroscientist, was also quoted in the article as saying, "At some point, clinging to a belief in God is just going to be too embarrassing."[2]

I think it is intriguing to think that this astute man, Sam, believes that "people of faith" can actually be embarrassed out of their faith. If we, as Christians, were holding to a belief that the world is flat when in fact it is round, maybe I could grasp what he is saying. But Christianity is essentially holding to a belief that the world is round when the rest of the world is claiming, in absolute ignorance, that it is, in fact, flat. Why should we be embarrassed about siding with the truth? Unless we ourselves aren't convinced that it is the truth. Bingo! This where the modern church is vulnerable, even to things as seemingly benign as, yes, embarrassment.

Pure and simple, we Christians are no longer convinced about what we believe.

If the true idea of faith isn't dismissed altogether within the church, then there is another chunk of the metrotheistic Christian world that has redefined it, making it a bit more palatable to the masses. Shockingly, right under our noses, the idea of faith has morphed into this odd and supremely *un*biblical notion of "an honest wavering in and out of belief." No longer is it being defined in accordance with Scripture as a certainty in God's promises, utter confidence in His ability to perform, and unwavering assuredness in His Word. And as a result, the modern crop of Christians are some of the most mealy-mouthed, waffling, uncertain, and beleaguered who have come along in the last 2000 years. We are so afraid of sounding overly certain and confident in our beliefs that it has almost become a newly christened and unwritten dogma that it is actually *more godly* for us as Christians to be unassuming in our expectations of God. It's now *more spiritual* to be uncertain of how He will perform on our behalf than to confidently proclaim what both we, and a dying world, can expect from the God of the Bible.

I've always referred to it as 51/49. If ever we arrive at the notion that something is true, we claim 51 percent assurance in the notion, which is offset by 49 percent doubt. And to be any more certain than 51 percent borders on spiritual presumption. After all, who are we to know the intentions of God?

Case in point: A high-profile Christian author received critical acclaim from a multitude of Christian leaders for his book on the topic of faith. This book was brilliantly written; however, I have never read a book within the confines of Christian thought that more acutely *undermined* the authentic moorings of the idea of faith. This well-known author, in his own self-prognosis, is "a pilgrim, septic with doubt."[3] And so his book on the topic of faith is merely the cynical musings of a wavering believer who is in and out of faith on a daily basis. Without a scrap of biblical support, the author redefined the entire construct of faith, basically terming it "honest doubt," or as he says, in his chapter entitled "Room for Doubt," "Doubt is the skeleton in the closet of faith, and I know no better way to treat a skeleton than to bring it into the open and expose it for what it is: not something to hide or fear, but a hard structure on which living tissue may grow." And then he continues on with, "Why, then does the church treat doubt as an enemy? I was once asked to sign *Christianity Today* magazine's statement of faith 'without doubt or equivocation.' I had to tell them I can barely sign my own name without doubt or equivocation."[4]

Am I to understand that what the Bible calls the *sin* of unbelief has now become an *ally* to the Christian faith? Is doubt really the skeletal structure on which the muscle and sinew of the body of Christ is intended to grow and thrive?

If this were just an obscure book selling a few thousand copies, I wouldn't lend it the time of day. But this book was crowned the Christian Book of the Year and has proven to be a defining instrument used in churches around the world to help struggling believers understand (or rather, misunderstand) what faith is and how it works.

Why is it that Christianity would turn to "a pilgrim, septic with doubt" to learn about the grand and glorious idea of faith? The aforementioned author himself admits to being hesitant to write about faith, for he is "afraid of causing someone else to lose theirs."[5] But instead of saying, "Thanks friend, for your honesty, but I would rather learn from someone who actually believes that God means what He says!" we lap it up like thirsty dogs because he is obviously one of the "good, honest" Christians and because he is enunciating precisely what we ourselves have so often experienced. We, the church, have become "pilgrims, septic with doubt," so this writer-guy is merely one of us. And his book on honest doubt resonates on a level that relates to where we're at.

But true faith doesn't just resonate with where we are at. It calls us out of our unbelief and onto a path of trust that will take us to places that we've never been.

E.M. Bounds, one of the most sturdy spectacles of faith in Christendom over the past few hundred years, said this:

> Doubt should never be cherished, nor fears harbored. Let none cherish the delusion that he is a martyr to fear and doubt. It is no credit to any man's mental capacity to cherish doubt of God, and no comfort can possibly derive from such a thought. Our eyes should be taken off self, removed from our own weakness

and allowed to rest implicitly upon God's strength. A simple, confiding faith, living day by day, and casting its burden on the Lord each hour of the day, will dissipate fear, drive away misgiving, and deliver from doubt.[6]

When I read E.M. Bounds, I am stirred. When I read Oswald Chambers, I am moved. When I read Charles Spurgeon, there is a rush of wind that blows upon the flame of my soul. And when I read A.W. Tozer I feel thunder, my heart quakes with conviction, and I am fueled with the desire to intimately know the holy God of the universe.

However, when I read the writer mentioned above, there is no sense of power. There is no sense of presence. There is no sense of passion. There is plenty of intellectual understanding of the problem, but little to no spiritual knowing of the solution. You sense that you are at the banks of Kadesh-barnea listening to one of the 12 spies return from his exhaustive investigation of the Promised Land only to say, "We can expect little from God in this situation, men. He is a governing force in our lives, but beyond manna, a cloud by day, and a pillar of fire by night, let's not get our expectations too high. After all, those Canaanite giants are ghastly large, and those walled cities reach high into the skies!" This Christian author is packing the same soul Novocain that led the Israelites to rot in the wilderness for 40 years—it's called good old-fashioned *doubt*.

Twenty

The Emergent Christian

The thing that really riles me about that *Wired* article is that these New Atheist guys are the ones who are standing up and stepping forward; they're the ones willing to draw a line in the sand and shout, "Who's in and who's out?!" (They obviously haven't lost their manly stuff over in that corner of the world.) But we as Christians are the ones called to contend for the faith. We are the ones who supposedly have a truth worth dying for. So, why in the world aren't we willing to raise the bar, to throw down the gauntlet in the church, and say, "Who's in and who's out?!"

According to a Christianpost.com article, "researchers found between 69-94 percent of Christian youths forsake their faith after leaving high-school. The Barna Group reported 64 percent loss after college graduation."[1] Those numbers are staggering! This is a mass exodus not *out* of Egypt, but *into* it. We are losing an entire generation. We have given them a watered-down frivolous gospel that in no way has impressed itself upon their souls. And for many, the first time someone ever drew a line in the sand and told them to choose this day whom they would serve was when they were sitting in a college classroom and an atheist professor got up in their face, with manly stuff intact, and barked about how crazy Christianity was, and how stupid they would be to dedicate the rest of their lives to something that doesn't even work. And you know what? The guy's right. If this is all there is to Christianity, then the thing is a joke!

I don't care if it's become popular within the corridors of the lukewarm, modern church to be loaded down with doubt, to question everything in Scripture, and to wonder if Gandhi may have had something equally as valid to say.[2] This treasonous mind-set may win accolades from the kingdom of darkness, but such blasphemy is considered the most grotesque rot in Heaven.

God is not looking for wafflers, fence-sitters, and double-minded philosopher types. In fact, He's bold enough in Revelation 3:16 to say He will spew such people out of His mouth (God's choice of words, not mine). God is looking for little children—children who simply trust that He means exactly what He says, and that He will do nothing less than what He has said He will do.

These young impressionable students are being asked to choose, they are being asked to radically believe, not by us Christians, but by militant atheists. They are being told, in no uncertain terms, that life and salvation is up to *them*. It's in our hands as humans to forge our own destiny. God isn't listening; He's not going to be helping. Because most of these young men and women grew up surrounded by "pilgrims, septic with doubt," it should be no surprise to find doubt toward God resident in their hearts and minds when they head off to college, where that doubt is played upon as if it were a Stradivarius violin.

If there can be a New Atheist, then I say let's call on a New Christian to stand up and grow a backbone. If a new sect of God haters is raising their voices, then I say let a new breed of Christians emerge out of their dusty tombs to display the resurrected power of the risen Christ to this dead and dying world! We need Christians who don't try to match God's words to their experience, but rather, whose experience is corrected, elevated, and altered by the Word's penetrating perfection. If we find ourselves cowering in unbelief at the words of our Master and Commander—if we are hiding behind rocks of doubt and unbelief on the shores of our soul—then I say it is high time that we stood up, squared our shoulders, dodged the bullets, and started charging in the direction of those "real life" cliffs.

THE BRAVEHEARTED PATH

LIVING MARTYRS

Most people today attempt to make a sales pitch for the gospel as if it were sweet plums and fairy dust, when it more accurately should be cast as an adventure full of blood, death, insurrection, trouble, persecution, and certain difficulty, with a shocking and ultra-dramatic final chapter in which the good guys win. In my opinion, this adventure dimension should be our sales pitch. Instead, the modern thought is "woo the masses in with Starbucks franchises stationed in the church lobby, movie-based sermons, beer and hot dog potlucks after the service, and the cool pelvic-thrust of a semi-moral garage band leading everyone into the worship of Jehovah God."

Christianity is the most explosive, most vibrant, most beautiful, most extraordinary news this universe has ever encountered, and yet all of us Christians are trying to make it more palatable. We are downplaying God's right to rule, overtake, and possess the lives of each and every person on this terrestrial ball. What might happen if we were to just let the gospel be what it is—a gritty, bloody, revolutionary call to die?

Everyone always says that they want to die in their sleep. Well, *I* don't want to die in my sleep. I don't want to get hit by a car and "go quickly without feeling a thing." I'm not saying that I wish to die of some gangrenous disease, withering away while people whisper among themselves, "It's just so sad!" But I have a hankering to die with heavenly gusto. I want to go out in a way that will bring a panicky uproar in Hell and a rousing applause in Heaven. *I want to die a martyr.*

I don't want to die for a cause, or a dream, or a movement, or a belief. I want to die for a Someone, and His name is Jesus.

I'm not a fan of pain any more than the average Joe. But I am probably a fan of Jesus more than the average Joe. And I simply want to give my life to Jesus in such a way that this world will be forced to take note of Him. All I care about is this Someone who has intoxicated my soul with effusive passion. I love Him so much it hurts with the most beautiful hurt.

I realize that my fascination with martyrdom might sound a bit odd to you. But, if we could take ourselves back to the first and second centuries of the church, we would be nodding along with understanding. In fact, every Christian back in those days was sharing in that dream to leave this Earth with heavenly panache. Dying a martyr's death was considered by all both the greatest honor and the single most powerful way to bring the power and love of the heavenly kingdom to this earth.[1]

I was reading about young Jim Hawkins last year in Robert Louis Stevenson's book *Treasure Island,* and I found myself asking the question, If I had a map for buried treasure, what would I do?

It's an interesting question to ponder.

I'm guessing most of you are thinking right now, *I'd go and dig it up!* I must admit that was my first thought, too. However, after much deliberation on this point, I've concluded that I don't think many of us, even with map in hand, would actually go.

Please don't be offended by my musing. It's just that I have a little background in this arena of "treasure," and I have found that the sheen of riches rubs off rather quick when the reality of what the expedition will cost becomes more apparent.

Digging up buried treasure sounds romantic, but when you get down to it, there are a lot of reasons to keep you at home and in the poorhouse. I mean, after all, you have to consider the daunting obstacles you will certainly face in such a journey:

- four months of seasickness and cabin fever
- rats and cockroaches as companions in your cabin

- evil pirates attempting to get to the treasure before you do, and willing to kill you to obtain your map (remember Long John Silver?)

- scurvy (the one disease that pirates always get)

- and then there is that nagging doubt that you have to carry throughout the whole journey, not knowing if this map is even genuine and accurate

My guess is that most of us wouldn't go because we like our comforts more than we crave adventure. We prefer our predictable ruts and addictions over the unpredictable nature of the unknown and unproven. It's an irony, but we will inevitably justify staying home because we will somehow convince ourselves that the cost is too great in order to obtain these riches untold.

If you have a Sunday school background, then you've probably heard the story of the Israelites standing on the shores of Kadesh-barnea and staring across the Jordan River into the land that God promised to give them. The land was right there in front of them. And the God of the universe was saying, "Go in and take it!"[2] But there were a few problems to take into account:

- This wasn't just a land of open empty meadows crying out for someone to rule over them. This was occupied territory. And of course, those who occupied it just happened to be of the giant-breed.

- Then there was the fact that this giant-breed was barricaded comfortably behind walled cities that reached up to the heavens (Deuteronomy 1:28).

- Oh, and we shouldn't forget the fact that the Israelites had just been freed from Egyptian slavery. These weren't fighting men; they were bricklayers. They didn't have fine weaponry, and they didn't have military order.

So the idea that God is proposing is a bit dubious at best. "Go in and take the land," He says. "Yeah, right!" squawks the nation of Israel. "Easy for you to say! You are all safe and secure up there in Heaven and you want us to take on thirty-one empires and bring down the giants!"

Why don't maps to buried treasure or promised land opportunities come with a bit more plausibility?

For instance, why couldn't a great grandfather pass away and leave a key to unlock a treasure trunk that's simply stored in his basement? That would be so much easier than those four months of seasickness and scurvy surrounded by swashbuckling pirates, not knowing the whole time if there will even be a treasure there.

Or why couldn't God just thunder down out of Heaven upon all 31 of these enemy empires and turn them to dust? Then there would be no need for fighting. Couldn't God quite easily make all the giants in the land die of gangrene so that Israel could just stroll on in and take what is theirs? Why does there have to be a challenge?

The gospel life is an adventure, plain and simple. It says in the Bible, "narrow is the way, which leadeth unto life, and few there be that find it."[3] The word "narrow" literally means "compressed, a path of pressure and difficulty." It's no wonder "*few* there be that find it."

We have emphasized comfort, stability, and earthly pleasure in the church for so long that we've forgotten what this whole ordeal is all about. It's about a King, *His* kingdom, and *His* glory!

The bravehearted path is all about dying to live, living to die! It's a violent and effusive love story between a Bridegroom and His bride, in which the Bridegroom radically spends His life to rescue His bride and then the bride, in turn, radically spends her life for the fame and renown of her Groom.

We have been given a map for buried treasure. In fact, it is a map for a treasure so extravagant and so priceless that it makes Jim Hawkins's chest of jewels look, in comparison, like a toy prize from a box of Cracker Jack.

But what good is a map unless we follow it, trust it, and abandon our lives to find that X that marks the spot?

To live for truth, you first must decide that you are willing to die for truth.

Doubt must be abandoned.

As Andrew the Apostle said to Governor Egeus, "I would not have preached the glory of the cross of Christ if I was first not willing to die upon it."[4]

Now, I don't know about you, but those don't sound like the words of a "pilgrim, septic with doubt" to me.

But how about us? What does Jesus mean to us? Is He just a fire insurance policy, or is He that Someone who has ravished our heart? Policies might get us into a church building, but they won't get us into Heaven. Jesus is looking for a bride, not a mere business partner.

The bravehearted path is all about drilling the seriousness, importance, and power of this Someone down into the bedrock of our souls. And when this Someone captivates our every thought, is infused into every action, and is interwoven into our every word spoken, then suddenly His passions become our passions.

The Bravehearted Gospel asks men and women to let go of their lives and grab hold of the life of Christ. It calls for us to radically trust the treasure map (aka Scripture) and spend our entire life, health, resources, and reputation to find what it's pointing toward. When this map says walk, we walk. When it says pick up the cross, we obey. When it says carry it, we yield. And when it says die upon it, then we die!

This is the gritty bravehearted path—this is the gritty reality of the cost of following Jesus.

If a Navy Seal, in his training, is being told to hold his breath under frigid ocean water for two minutes, he doesn't look back at his drill instructor and scream, "That's not fair! My friend Johnny, who's a private in the army, has never been asked to do that!"

A Navy Seal realizes the opportunity it is to be trained at such an elite level within the armed forces. To be chosen to train as a Navy Seal is an honor, not a burden. And it is an honor that every Navy Seal applied for, prayed for, campaigned for, and labored for. Long and short, it is the privilege of a lifetime. So when he is dunked under those frigid waters, he's not moaning with self-pity, but is inwardly ecstatic that he is being offered the opportunity to follow the path and join the ranks of the Navy Seals who have gone before him.

Christianity is an invitation into a regal fellowship. It is an inauguration into a throng of the most princely and radiant to ever walk this earth. Is it easy? *By no means.* But is it worth it? *Absolutely.* It is, as the church in South America says, *vale la pena*—it's worth all the pain.

We are being asked to bear the holy name of Jehovah upon our being. Do we not realize that this means we will be treated in the same manner He was treated? Do we not realize what Christianity actually is? It's an invitation into the life, love, *and sufferings* of our beautiful King.

God is looking for those who won't bemoan the call of Christ but will gladly follow the Lamb wherever He may go. God is looking for men and women with a Navy Seal-like outlook, who won't complain about the physical, mental, or spiritual challenges that He may bring while fully equipping them for battle. He's looking for men like Paul, who will rejoice[5] in such training, for they have been chosen to work side by side with the very Someone who has ravished their heart and intoxicated their souls with a mighty and effusive passion.

God is looking for not just men and women who will spend their life in death, but men and women who will spend their life radically every moment while they are still yet alive. The eyes of our Lord are searching to and fro throughout the earth for those who will join his army of living martyrs.

The name of Christ, the purpose of Christ, and the person of Christ is being diminished in the corridors of the modern church. What should a living martyr do?

The Word of God is being diluted, paraphrased, altered, and perverted by those who claim to represent our Jesus. What should a living martyr do?

The gospel of salvation is being altered, abandoned, and emptied of its grit and glory. What should a living martyr do?

There are 143 million orphans in the world without a father and without the gospel.

There are more people living in slavery today than at any other time in world history.

There are little boys in Uganda being forced to kill their parents and who are then forced into the army to make killing their daily chore.

What should a living martyr do?

There are millions of street children in Latin America, vulnerable to death squads that hunt them down and kill them for sport like rats.

There are five-year-old little girls being sold into slave prostitution, whose bodies are being broken, battered, and abused. And there is no one who hears their cries for help.

There are more people alive today who don't know Jesus than ever before. They are lost and hellbound.

What should a living martyr do?!

We have grown up amidst a church that sends its money but doesn't send itself. We have grown up amidst a form of religion that protects itself and never spends itself. But is this a church like its Founder, who, at the greatest cost to Himself, came to seek and save that which was lost?

The stuff of the Bravehearted Gospel is the stuff of frontline soldiers. It's the stuff of martyrs and mighty men.

The stuff of the Bravehearted Gospel is the stuff of the eleventh chapter of Hebrews: It's men and women who through faith subdue kingdoms, bring righteousness, obtain promises, and stop the mouths of lions. It's men and women who quench the violence of fire, escape the edge of the sword. It's men and women who out of weakness are made strong, wax valiant in fight, and turn to flight the armies of the aliens.

Hebrews 11 says of these that many of these men and women were tortured and yet would not accept deliverance in order that they might obtain a better resurrection. Even others endured the trial of cruel mockings and scourgings, and endured chains and imprisonment. They were stoned, they were sawn in half, were tempted, were slain with the sword; they wandered about in sheepskins and goatskins, being destitute, afflicted, tormented.

But what does God say of these extraordinary men and women?

That this world was not worthy of them.

They were built with the sacred substance of Heaven, which for some reason, is always rejected down here on Earth.

The manly stuff inside of me salivates for such a life of grand adventure. And I for one long to be "sawn in half" if Jesus Christ would be seen more clearly in and through my sacrifice. By God's grace I will embrace my own death if He says to me, "Eric, please do it for My glory." May every cell within this body, known as Eric Ludy, yield itself to the purposes of Jesus Christ.

May the name of Jesus be exalted, the Word of God protected, the gospel of God proclaimed, the life of Christ preached with boldness and unfettered conscience, the orphan and the widow heroically rescued, the enslaved radically set free, the street children preserved by our bodies taking the bullets, the boy soldiers set free to be children again because we purloined them from enemy hands, and may those little prostituted five-year-old girls find that they have a muscular advocate in *us*—even at the cost of our very lives. May we be willing to claw through concrete walls with our bare hands, if necessary, to see them safe in the arms of grace.

I don't know about you, but this is the life that I desire. A Christ-life, a life of hero work, a life with the bravehearted crest tattooed on my forehead. I want to dive into the fray and set some fur a-flying.

Who's with me?

Part Five

The Bliss of Unknowing

Cultivating ignorance to evade obedience

Twenty-one

AVOIDING TRUTH
TO BECOME LIKE GOD

In college, my roommate Bob and I both had really smelly athlete's feet. I was a soccer player, he was a swimmer, and our dorm room wasn't the most pleasant place as a result. Bob's dad prescribed the ultimate cure-all for our problem. The directions went something like this: one part water, three parts bleach. Or was it, three parts water and one part bleach? Bob couldn't quite remember which one it was. But he declared, "All I know, Ludy, is bleach will totally kill off athlete's foot!" So we decided to go with the "one part water, three parts bleach" option.

As the story goes, Bob and I entered the men's bathroom confident. While sitting up on the bathroom counter, we unveiled our stinky feet and submerged them into the "one part water, three part bleach" mixture awaiting us in the sink basins.

It wasn't but three minutes later that I asked Bob, "How long do we need to do this?"

"My dad said twenty minutes," he responded with certainty.

My feet were burning. They actually felt hot. This was very uncomfortable, but if Bob could handle it, then I wasn't about to be the big baby.

Bob and I were turning various shades of pink at about minute five. It was at about this point when Bob muttered something like, "I'm guessing ten minutes would probably be enough!"

I quickly agreed with a moan. My feet were flaming hot and a bright red color.

As the minutes passed I refused to pull my feet out before Bob did. Come to find out later, he refused to pull his feet out until I did. I'm guessing we made it nearly six minutes before one of us cracked. Since I'm the one writing the story, we'll just say that it was Bob.

Even though we removed our feet from this wicked substance, the pain still remained. We rinsed our feet under cold water for the next half hour and the pain continued. It was miserable. Every last hair on my feet was literally burned off. Nothing remained. Even an inch up my leg, all the hair was just gone! Poof!

Come to find out, the recipe was supposed to be something like *ten* parts water and one part bleach. Talk about miscommunication! The hair did eventually grow back, but still, I've never let Bob live it down.

———

When I was 18 my view of truth was quite similar to my view of Bob's cure-all formula for athlete's foot. Sure, bleach may kill athlete's foot, but it should be administered and experienced only at seriously diluted levels.

I know this might sound strange, but when I was 18 I was desperately afraid of being "overeducated" in my faith. My attitude was that the Bible was a book to be respected, but one must always be careful not to get all caught up in the specifics of what it says. I was paranoid about joining the "soundness of doctrine" craze. In fact, theology and doctrine were painted up in my mind as antispiritual in nature.

Here's a quote that I remember from my past: "Those people who are all fixated on parsing Scripture and knowing verb tenses miss the whole point of the gospel!"

I don't know who I heard this from, but it is a very clear, reverberating idea from my adolescent years. In fact, I'm afraid that if someone had preached a sermon back then on "the satanic agenda to get Christians to fixate on theology and doctrine," I would have yelled out a hearty amen.

I've talked with a lot of young people in my generation who have shared a similar paranoia. Somehow, a message started floating around inside the church that basically said, "Soundness of doctrine equates to dullness of life."

In actuality, this message is nothing less than the serpent's lie to Eve restated in modern terms.

Eve: "But God said that we shouldn't eat of this fruit, and that if we eat of it we would surely die."

Serpent: "Oh, come on, Eve, surely you aren't so immature in your relationship with your heavenly Father as to believe that He would literally *kill* you if you disobeyed Him, are you?"

Eve: "Well, He *did* say that we *would* die."

Serpent: "You need to be really careful here, Eve. You seem to be getting too hung up on words and definitions, and I think that you're missing the spirit of the matter. God's words are deep and can have many different meanings; and you never want to make the simplistic mistake of turning them into legalistic, literalistic dogma. After all, you can't just put God in a box. The truth is, this fruit will actually make you *more* like God. Don't you want to be more like God, Eve? Don't you think that would be a *good* thing?"

Can you believe that Eve, much less anyone else, falls for this garbage? Ignore God's word, pay no attention to what He said. In fact, do the exact opposite of what He said, and in the end you will somehow, miraculously become *more* like God. Ridiculous!

But millions have, and millions do fall for this crazy idea that by avoiding the practical, literal, real-world truths of Scripture they are in some way more spiritual than those who are "bogged down in doctrine." I should know; I believed it for years! And as a result, I was a religious illiterate. And here's the odd part: I was actually proud of this! I honestly felt like I was closer to the "heart" of God in not having all that biblical head knowledge cluttering up my simple love for Jesus. I was "experiencing" God in my heart and not merely "deducing" Him in my head like so many of those "high-minded" Christians did. And it's not that I was an idiot—I was academically strong in all my classes in college. It's simply that I was duped into believing doctrine was like bleach—the more you mix in, the more painful life will be.

Whether I knew it or not, I was living with an overwhelmingly unhealthy dose of the feminine emphasis on feeling and intuition while the masculine balancing emphasis on the accuracy of truth and the preservation of sound doctrine was treated as a grave error that was to be avoided like the plague.

I was sitting in a Bible conference one day when I was 19. This round-faced theologian type got up in front of the class and started hollering about why we must be sound in our doctrine. I instinctively stiffened. I instantly looked at this character with a wary eye. I figured he was one of those intellectual kinds of Christians, probably stuffy in his mind and empty in his heart.

I attempted to label this man an intellectual stiff, but his message was cutting into my heart and impacting my inner man. In fact, as he spoke, it was like spiritual lightning to my soul. His ideas were sound, and they didn't squash the life of the gospel. In fact, what surprised me is that the soundness seemed to enhance the life.

Note: This is the pattern of Scripture, and the pattern of the Bravehearted Gospel—soundness is intended by God *to fortify* life, *not* to make it hollow and empty.[1]

My view on the Bible has so completely transformed since my freshman year of college. I honestly feel like I'm writing about someone else when I talk about my past struggles with Bible paranoia.

Now I spend quite a large chunk of my time training young Christian leaders in the importance, the substance, and the immeasurable power of the Word of God (now isn't that an irony only a Christian mother would love). In fact, every few months from all over the world, twenty-somethings travel to Windsor, Colorado, and we get down to business—the serious business of discipleship. I forewarn them that it will be intense, uncomfortable at times, and a superlative challenge. For three straight days we venture through the Word of God. For three straight days we measure our lives up against the sterling perfection of Scripture. And for three straight days we squirm, writhe, and contort until we finally come to grips with the fact that we are completely unlike the substance of this grand book. We are in need of the Author of this grand book to elevate us to walk worthy of our calling. And even though our souls work up quite a sweat, we find this is actually fun! Because encountering Scripture doesn't leave you dull and dour, but rather, broken, rebuilt, and fully alive!

I absolutely adore Scripture. I often spend upwards of three hours during a given day just basking in the beauty, majesty, and power of the Bible. To me the Bible is not an antiquated, outdated collection of thoughts and ideas. To me the Bible is alive. Its ideas are potently relevant and supernaturally charged and equipped to change, alter, and totally transform not just my life, but your life, the church, and this entire world if we would all merely submit to follow its guidance.

The Bible is amazingly flawless. I'm not saying that the individual translations of it are not intermixed with the errant input of men. Rather, I'm saying the Bible, in its native substance, is without spot or wrinkle— it is a supernatural compilation of 66 awe-inspiring books. And when I read it, study it, and meditate on it, I fully expect to encounter the God of the universe afresh. It's like a porthole into the inner sanctum of the divine.

The substance of this supernatural book is Jesus. He is the Word of God. And when you explore the vast text of Scripture, you find that every word, every sentence, every paragraph, every chapter, and every book is fraught with the nature, the person, the purpose, and the perfection of Jesus Christ. It's literally all about Him—life with Him, life without Him, life in Him, and His life in us.

I could go on and on. I honestly find my greatest delight in encountering Jesus in and through His Word. I believe that every nook and cranny of His Word to be completely true—and that it is true for today. And trust me, I fully recognize the fact that my view of the Bible is considered rather odd as of late. In fact, Pastor Bell from Grand Rapids, Michigan, in his book *Velvet Elvis*, has the gall to refer to this view of the Bible as "toxic and warped."[2]

Most Christians "respect" the Bible, but very few, in the West at least, treat it as precious, drink in its every word as if it were dew from heaven, and cherish its every thought as though it were, in fact, divine.

Most Christians know little bits and pieces of the Bible, but few spend their lives getting familiar with every last nuance of it.

Most Christians believe it is generally trustworthy, but few are willing to bank everything on what it says.

Our archenemy, Satan, has always had it in for the Word of God. His goal, from the beginning, has been to remove its credibility, diminish its value, twist its words, and ultimately empty it of its power. In the Garden of Eden, he slithered onto the scene whispering, "Did God *really* say?"[3]

Well, this strategy of the enemy has obviously proven quite effective over the centuries, because, as I pointed out earlier, that is precisely what he is still whispering.

"Are you sure that it was *God* who put this whole Bible together? Are you completely certain that this whole Scripture thing isn't just a compilation of good ideas written by good men?"

"Did God really intend for you to take all this Bible stuff so literally? I mean, come on—if you took that statement right there literally, you would be penniless and friendless in less than one month."

"Did God really mean for you to apply these ancient ideas to our modern world? Are you sure these weren't all just answers to specific cultural dilemmas people faced back in that particular time period?"

Satan's whispering is relentless, and it all centers on one very important theme: the credibility of the Bible. And you can always tell when this agenda has proven effective in someone's life, because it causes Christians to backpedal when they are asked to defend the Bible. It causes them to get sheepishly awkward and mumble things like, "Well, I'm not saying that everything in it is correct." When Satan is having his way, Christians spend their time making excuses for the Bible instead of living out the substance inside of it.

Twenty-two

ERIC, THE INTERPRETER

I personally have lacked the manly emphasis on the accuracy of truth and the preservation of sound doctrine for most of my Christian life. For years I explained away large segments of the Bible under the banner of being a "wise" and "astute" handler of God's Word. I used terms such as *cultural context* and *the spirit of the text* to the point where I began to believe that those terms were actually used by Christ Himself.

"Well, you have to be careful with *that* Scripture," I would say with an understanding nod and a kind smile. "Taking it literally could lead to all sorts of problems. God is more interested in you living out the spirit of those words."

Come on, Eric! Be a man! Allow Scripture to say what it says; get out of the way and let God speak! If He is saying, "Charge!" don't reason it away and say, "Well, He obviously didn't mean for us to charge into the line of fire. We could get killed doing that! So let's just live out the 'spirit' of that command and 'charge' inwardly toward the high cliffs of our soul while hiding behind this nice big rock of unbelief over here."

By doing that, I am guilty of being an *interpreter* of the Bible instead of a *preacher* of the Word.

Someone would ask me, "Eric, what do you think Jesus means in Matthew chapter six when He says, 'take no thought' for your life? Because He says it like three times over and over again, like He means it!"

At this I would squirm a bit, maintaining my calm demeanor the entire time.

"Well, Missy," I would say, implementing my confident counseling voice, "again we need to look at the *spirit* of what Christ is saying there!"

"Well," Missy would continue, "if we are always taking only the *spirit* of what Christ is saying, is there ever a time to actually *do* exactly what He says?"

In the first ten years of my ministry I found myself, unwittingly, looking at the Bible through a lens that would justify my version and my level of spirituality, rather than allowing it to *reform* my version and *upgrade* my level of spirituality.

"It says here in Matthew 4:5," Missy would say, "that we are to give to whomever asks. Are we supposed to look at the spirit of that too, Eric?"

"Well [cough]," I would mutter, "that particular passage [cough], uh, is quite an interesting one."

Come on, Eric! Grow a backbone! Since I personally didn't give to everyone who asked of me, how could I uphold the actual words of Christ and tell others to do it? And this is what Christian leaders do day in and day out.

Well, I'm still addicted to pornography and subject to the impulses of lust, they reason to themselves, *so how can I say that God will deliver the people in my church from similar vices?*

I'm in deep financial debt and totally subservient to the world's financial system, they inwardly ponder, *so how in the world can I "take no thought" for my life and tell all the other indebted people in my church to do the same?*

We are bringing the words of Christ down to match our experience rather than expecting the God of the Bible to raise our experience up to match His astounding Word!

Twenty-three

WIKIBIBLIA

I t is currently in vogue to treat the Bible as merely a narrative (aka a great story). Brian McLaren, one of the more prominent leaders of the emergent movement, has made this narrative idea fashionable in our modern times.[1]

Here's a conversation I had with a young man just the other day:

"I'm concerned, Eric, that you are taking the Bible a bit too literally."

"How's that?"

"Well, you end up stuck in the legalism of fundamentalism if you actually think that God intends for us to live all of these specific commands out in the real world."

"Are you proposing that it is legalism to obey God?"

"I think it is legalism to treat the Bible in that manner. The Bible is more of a narrative. It's not an objective declaration of absolute truth."

"What do you mean when you say it's more of a narrative?"

"Well, it's basically a story that has good ideas, noble themes, and solid moral substance. And if we use simple wisdom, we can implement the heart of this story into our modern world. In other words, we can learn to be kind, forgiving, and generally peace-loving."

The entire time he was talking I was thinking to myself, *Ah, a McLarenite!* I can spot them a mile away. Now, I too am a fan of being kind, forgiving, and generally peace-loving, but not at the expense of truth. Why is it that taking the Bible to mean exactly what it says is now considered dangerous? Why is it considered a threat? Because, these narrative folks much prefer the idea of defining truth to be whatever they wish to make it as opposed to what God has already defined it to be.

Wikipedia is a giant online encyclopedia that started off as a blank Web site and grew as people added entries to it. It is an encyclopedia that each and every reader can edit as they see fit. Definitions on Wikipedia are really just placeholders until someone who thinks they have a better understanding of a given subject comes along and edits it. So, in reality, nothing is "defined" on Wikipedia. Rather, everything is in the constant process of being defined and then redefined by the community that uses it.

For McLaren, Bell, the emergent church, and so many others, the Bible is a lot more like Wikipedia than the timeless, unchanging bastion of truth that it is. For them, the Bible isn't really the revealed Word of God that *provides* definitions *to* us as much as it is something that provides *us* with opportunities to create definitions for ourselves.

Rob Bell, for instance, makes no bones about it, but clearly states in his book *Velvet Elvis* that the writings within the Bible are not "first and foremost timeless truths." He goes on further to say that Jesus gave to us, His followers, the authority to "make new interpretations of the Scriptures," and that "the Bible is open-ended."[2]

In other words, the Bible is really just a giant, ancient wiki. *Wikibiblia* we'll call it. Run across a particular entry you don't like? No problem— just edit it. And as long as enough people in the community agree with your redefinition, then your edit will become the "new truth" that will be read and imbibed by the masses. At least, that is, until someone else comes along and edits your entry. Then that edit will become the "new truth" and so on, and so on. In this way we have "truth" constantly evolving with the culture, and Wikibiblia being ceaselessly updated and revised to keep up with the times and therefore staying fresh, and most importantly, relevant.

This is nothing more than truth by the vote of the people, truth by numbers, truth by consensus. And in the end, it is no truth at all.

The Bible is none of the above. The Bible is truth by revelation. It is God's Word revealing His will to humanity. And we are not its editors; we are its servants!

The apostle Peter said,

> Knowing this first, that no prophecy of the scripture is of any private interpretation. For the prophecy came not in old time

by the will of man: but holy men of God spake as they were moved by the Holy Ghost.[3]

The narrative folk want us to believe that if we let the Bible just say what it says, that we very well might end up with more religious crusades and inquisitions.[4] When in actuality, letting the Bible say exactly what it says leads to love, joy, peace, patience, kindness, goodness, faithfulness, gentleness, and self-control. It leads to Jesus—the love of Jesus, the power of Jesus, the kingdom of Jesus, and the glory of Jesus lived out in the hearts and lives of holy women and men the world over!

Quite to the contrary, it was precisely because of men trying to edit the Bible in order to make it back their own twisted agendas that led to the Crusades and Inquisitions in the first place.

If I were to translate this conflict over the Bible into a political dialogue between superpowers, it would sound sort of like this:

Dear Bible-thumpers,

It has come to our attention that you are continuing to harbor sentiments of brainwashing the known world into believing that there is only one way to God. However, we too are also Christians and are deeply offended by the arrogance with which you have chosen to portray the Christian faith to the world. It is also our understanding that you are still withholding your support for our unilateral peace accords and continue to refuse to participate in our proposed disarmament treaty. This is most alarming. For we recognize, in these actions, your intent to retain within your arsenal that weapon of mass destruction which all peace-loving nations have agreed to disarm and mothball—*the Bible*. These actions are very irresponsible and unfeeling toward your fellowman, knowing good and well the mass discomfort, guilt, and all-around misery that would follow in the wake of such a weapon being detonated. Now, we don't mind you possessing this "nuclear bomb." We just plead that you would have the sanity to disarm it, point it away from all peace-loving people, and keep it stored out of sight and out of mind. For as long as you continue to flaunt international opinion by training the sights of this great weapon upon the entire civilized world, there will be unrest and unease among our populations. We really don't wish to be negative or unconstructive in our criticism, so we've included below a few suggestions as to how you could use this deadly resource in a manner that is more beneficial to society. For instance, many in our countries have found a wide variety of creative purposes for utilizing "the bomb's" many intricate internal components. Some have even entertained large crowds by juggling its most explosive parts while riding a unicycle across a tightrope. Also, many have found great fun in dancing around the radioactive pieces, all the while trying desperately not to touch them. In other words, have fun with it. Let's not think thoughts of war, but of peace. So please, for the sake of civility, order, and societal decorum, lighten up! Deconstruct your bomb, and then everyone can breathe a sigh of relief.

Yours truly,

The Bible-massagers

The Bible has become clay in the hands of a million potters. And these potters are currently shaping it to say whatever they desire it to say. But, whether our flesh likes it or not, the Bible is saying the same thing today that it has always said. It doesn't "evolve,"[5] as Brian McLaren would have us believe. It doesn't stretch to fit our whim and agenda, as Rob Bell would have us think. Rather, the Bible, like its Great Author, is the same yesterday, today, and forever.[6] And like its Author, "in it is no shadow of turning."[7]

Let me get something off my chest: The Bible *does* have *great stories* in it, but the Bible is much more than stories. The Bible is more than mere literature. It is more than letters on a page. It is the mind, heart, and love of Jesus Christ made available for us to enjoy, drink in, soak up, bask in, and fully know.

I realize that I've poured it on pretty thick here. Obviously I'm harboring a bit of pent-up emotion in this particular arena of thought. But as my hero Leonard Ravenhill once said, "My Lord is insulted and His church slighted. And believe me, under this double injury, I smart. The church has many adversaries. Can my sword sleep, then, in my hand? Never!"[8]

The issue of the Bible is a battleground. It's an issue of God's glory that is at stake. And the man inside of me just can't sit back and let the power of my God be diminished. For if the integrity of the Bible is lost, then everything it claims about the person, the plans, the purposes, and the power of God are then equally lost, flushed down the rusty drainpipe of ignorance.

———

I realize we all have our moments of stupidity. We grow up with intellectual blind spots that expose themselves at the most inopportune times. Like that one moment in my freshman year of college when the topic of John F. Kennedy, Jr. came up in conversation with all my buddies.

"Did you hear that he flunked the bar exam for the third time?" my friend, Paul, muttered incredulously.

This was my moment to shine. I barged into the conversation with all my ignorance on full display and asked, "Why is someone with the connections he has even studying to be a bartender in the first place?"

As I said, I realize that we all have our moments of stupidity. But, if I'm not mistaken, it seems to me that the modern church isn't just struggling with intellectual blindspots, but with intellectual blind*ness*.

We've grown stupid. We have lost our reverence and respect for the Bible, and in one fell swoop, we have also lost our spiritual brains. I'm not a big fan of "blonde jokes," but I have to admit if there was ever a time when the church was vulnerable to having all those blonde jokes translate into "stupid Christian jokes," it would be now.

We no longer have that manly passion for the accuracy of truth and the preservation of sound doctrine. We no longer are willing to wage war for the glory of God. We no longer stand like Athanasius *contra mundum* when the integrity of truth is threatened by the powers that be. We are no longer shouting, "No quarter!" to the flesh and seeking to stamp out every brushfire of self-indulgence and lethargy. Instead, we are often unwittingly standing *with* the world *against* the truth of the Bible, decrying it as prejudiced and shortsighted, intolerant and legalistic.

We are allowing anything and everything into the church these days. We are no longer letting the manly stuff defend our frontiers and borders. And it's not just the vulgar stuff that is being carted in by the ton—it's the doctrines that applaud honest doubt, the doctrines that esteem self, the doctrines that worship culture, the doctrines that encourage worldliness, and the doctrines that redefine God to be something that He simply isn't.

Not many would fault the modern church for being unloving these days, but unloving is *exactly* what we are. For if we truly *loved* God, we would obey Him (John 14:21). If we truly *loved* the church, we would labor to keep it unstained and unmolested by this world (James 1:27). And if we truly *loved* the lost, we would introduce them to the God of the Bible who is able to save their souls, and not the pitiful god of our own making who is having a hard time saving anything at all (Psalm 50:21).

Remember the treasure map we talked about a few chapters back? Well, the Bible *is* our treasure map. And if this map is altered, then the treasure can no longer be found. There's a simple principle when it comes to treasure maps: mess with them, and you mess with the treasure itself. Lose them, and you lose the fortune to which they point. Lose even a tiny piece of them, and often the entire treasure will be lost.

Treasure hunting isn't a complicated business, but it is a dangerous one. Remember those evil pirates who are out to strip you of your map and kill you before you ever reach that X that marks the spot? Well, believe me, they're out there. And every evil pirate in Hell wants that map stripped out of your hands and to see your soul floating facedown in the ocean. They know how valuable that treasure map is, but very few Christians today realize how truly priceless is that bloodstained parchment that is so often left to do nothing but gather dust on a shelf.

The bravehearted Christian life isn't just about standing for something and being willing to die for it; it's also about knowing what to stand for and what to die for. And throughout history, the treasure map—the Bible—has been one of the number one things that the heroes of the faith have been willing to pour out their lives to preserve and protect.

This map is of inestimable value not because it is the treasure, but because it is the only thing in this world that can help us find the treasure.

And the treasure is none other than Jesus Christ, the living, breathing, risen, Son of God Himself! And as a result, we must treat this map as the single most important physical item on God's green Earth. How we treat it is a statement of how we are treating Jesus Christ Himself. Because when you mess with the map, you mess with the treasure itself.

Flavius Josephus, a Jewish historian who lived during the time of Jesus, wrote,

> We [the Jews] have given practical proof of our reverence for our own Scriptures. For, although such long ages have now passed, no one has ventured either to add, or to remove, or to alter a syllable; and it is an instinct with every Jew, from the day of his birth, to regard them as the decrees of GOD, to abide by them, and, if need be, cheerfully to die for them. Time and again ere now the sight has been witnessed of prisoners enduring tortures and death in every form in the theatres, rather than utter a single word against the laws and the allied documents.[9]

Could we in the body of Christ today say, with our integrity intact, that "although such long ages have now passed, no one in the church has ventured either to add, or to remove, or to alter a syllable" of the Bible? Could we with any integrity say that we train Christians from the day of their birth to regard holy Scripture as the decrees of God, to abide by them, and if need be, cheerfully to die for them? Sadly, we have fallen a great distance from such a mentality.

The Jewish people were entrusted with the words of God and gave their lives to protect them. We as Christians have not only been entrusted with the words of God, but with the Word of God made flesh as well, and yet we often treat those words as if they were a really cool $1 T-shirt that we scavenged from the racks at Goodwill.

I plead with you to consider joining me in once again placing a manly emphasis on the accuracy of truth and the preservation of sound doctrine. We must learn to treat Scripture with even a greater deference than even the Jews did. We must tremble before the Bible, protect its integrity, and guard its every jot and tittle as if they were the fingers and toes of Jesus Christ Himself.

Here's what the apostle John had to say on the subject:

> I testify unto every man that heareth the words of the prophecy of this book, If any man shall add unto these things, God shall add unto him the plagues that are written in this book: And if any man shall take away from the words of the book of this prophecy, God shall take away his part out of the book of life, and out of the holy city, and from the things which are written in this book.[10]

———

Let's take a quick look at how the Jews handled the treasure map. I believe you will find this not only fascinating, but deeply convicting.

This is the stuff of the bravehearted.

Back in first century A.D., the transcription of holy Scripture, amongst the Hebrew people, was handled by the Jewish Talmudists. To them, Scripture was a "Sacred of sacred" article, words given to the Jewish people by God Himself. And they trembled at the task of even transferring it from one scroll to another, for fear that they would omit a single word or alter a jot or tittle. There were 17 specific things that a Talmudist was trained to do when transcribing the holy text, and if even one of these 17 things was overlooked, the entire text would be determined false and it would be buried or burned lest it accidently be treated as if it were the true canon of God.

Here are a few of the 17 sacred requirements:

- The animal skin (or roll) upon which the Scripture would be copied must be from a clean animal (one without spot or defect).

- Every animal skin used for this sacred purpose must contain an exact number of columns, and this number must be kept perfectly constant throughout the entire copying process.

- The length of each column must not be less than 48 lines and not exceed 60 lines; and the breadth of each column must consist of exactly 30 letters.

- The whole copy must first be lined to maintain horizontal exactitude; and if even three words be written without a line, the entire copy is treated as worthless.

- The ink used for the copy must be black (neither red, green, nor any other color can be utilized), and the black ink must be prepared according to a very specific recipe.

- The Talmudist must copy the text from an already authenticated "canonized" transcription of Scripture, and from this canonized copy the transcriber must not in the least deviate.

- The Talmudist is forbidden to write down one word or letter, even a yod, out of his memory. He must always copy from the canon exactly as it is, and he must not ever allow his "perception of what the canon states" to affect his transcription.

- Between every consonant the space of a hair or thread must intervene; between every new parashah, or section, the breadth of nine consonants; between every book, three lines. The fifth book of Moses must terminate exactly with a line; but the rest of the canon books need not do so. These measurements must be kept constant.

- The Talmudist copyist must transcribe only while in full Jewish dress.

- He must wash his whole body and freshly clean his pen before ever daring to write the holy name of God, and should a king address him while writing that name he must take no notice of him.[11]

If the 17 regulations of the Talmudist were not observed to the smallest detail, then the roll upon which the Talmudist was transcribing would be deemed condemned and buried in the ground or burned (or sometimes, depending on the degree of variance, these copies were banished to the schools as an unauthorized transcription for reading). Yet if the 17 regulations were adhered to with perfection, then, when the copy was finished, it was treated as an exact duplicate and the new copy was given equal canon authority and authorized to be itself used for the purposes of duplication.

I am shamed by such reverence for Scripture. It shocks me to think how far we have come, in the church, from this "Talmudist trembling." And what is even more terrifying is that, as Paul says in 2 Corinthians 3:3, we are called to be living epistles. In other words, we are to be

Talmudic copies of Scripture for this world to read in the living color of human flesh and blood.

But we never even consider the fact that such words cannot be written on unclean skins. They cannot be written with the ink of self-ambition, self-reliance, and self-glory, but rather, only with the ink of God's Spirit in accordance with the very specific recipe spelled out in Scripture. So many of us are "false" renditions of God's Word. And it's sad to say, but a good Talmudist would be trained to either burn or bury "such renditions." We are not accurate representations, and we have not carried into the copying process the reverent bearing of a Talmudist, but rather the cavalier attitude of a modern Christian. Do we not realize that we are writing the holy name of Jehovah with our very lives, attitudes, and actions?

Let me add insult to injury by sharing a bit more Jewish history:

Whereas the Talmudists were responsible for copying the text, it was a special class of Jewish men known as the Massoretes (in the sixth century A.D.) who were selected to take the Talmudist's work and standardize it. The Jewish Talmudist text didn't have any vowels, so one of the Massoretes's responsibilities was to add vowels into the sacred body to ensure proper pronunciation. Like the Talmudist, the Massoretes had an elaborate process that they subjected themselves to in their work. This process consisted of complicated and intricate safeguards in order to ensure that the biblical writing was handled with sacred dexterity and that not even one error would enter into the text. (Note: This Massoretic text is the standard Hebrew text today.)

The Massoretes would count the number of times each letter of the alphabet occurred within each book, and they marked the middle letter of the Pentateuch and the middle letter of the entire Hebrew Bible. These calculations, as well as hundreds more, the Massoretes practiced continually. And while these calculations may seem to us today as absurd and unnecessary trivialities, they were done out of the highest regard for the ancient text. For these elaborate calculations served as an "integrity check" against which the Massoretes could test the perfection of each new transcription, maintaining the strictest guard on the sacred accuracy of every word.[12] The Massoretes were reverently fearful and did not want one jot nor tittle, not a single letter nor one minuscule part of a letter of the law, to pass away or be lost.[13]

Please forgive this brief Jewish history lesson, but I felt it was necessary in order to demonstrate how far we have diverged today from such a pattern in our veneration for the integrity and accuracy of Scripture. We've lost that bravehearted yearning to fight for what is sacred and to die for what is at the center of God's heart.

Is it just me, or does it seem that we in the church have become spiritual slackers? We want all the blessings of Heaven, but we don't feel that we should do anything to get them. If we were to be honest, if the Talmudists and the Massoretes were still around today, the modern church would brand them legalists.

"Those Talmudists need to loosen up and have some fun!" I can hear a modern Christian say.

"God isn't so concerned about every little jot and tittle!" someone else might declare. "He's merely interested in the vibe of Scripture coming across."

Men and women throughout history have given up their lives to preserve the integrity of jots and tittles, so I say, "Let's honor that blood that's been shed!" Because it was shed for a reason. The Bible is not simply a narrative that we can edit at whim and will. Neither is it a smorgasbord from which we can pick and choose, taking only the sweets and pastries but, like spoiled children, leaving everything that doesn't suit our tastes to be fed to the dogs.

You personally might not see any value in a particular jot or a tittle, but God does, and for those of a bravehearted soul, that is all that matters.

THE BRAVEHEARTED PATH

THE CANON-MIND

I n chapter 14 we discussed a mind-set that I referred to as an open mind. It sounds all good and well to have an open mind—after all, what are your options otherwise? A closed mind? A narrow mind? No thanks! But, whereas having an open mind toward all things godly is a wonderful thing, the kind of open mind being propagated within the church today is an open mind to anything and everything. It's all-accepting, tolerant of all thoughts, opinions, ideas, and religions. Our culture loves this kind of thinking, but God detests it.

I love my marriage. I love my wife, Leslie. And in step with my ardent love, I am a faithful, attentive, and adoring husband. My point is that ardent love leads to ardent loyalty. I love Jesus. And in step with my ardent love for my King, I give up my mind, my heart, and my body for Him to define according to the pattern of His kingdom. I am exclusively His. And therefore, it is His thoughts, His ideas, and His manner that shapes me—nothing else. In fact, it would be considered prostitution of my heart and mind if I were to give this world and its religions equal opportunity to define my life and worldview. I made the choice long ago that if anything—no matter how true it may sound—violates the words of my King as revealed in Scripture, I will treat it as the most dangerous lie.

If I, with bald-faced arrogance, went out and slept around with every attractive girl whom I met, how do you think Leslie would feel? That's right—her heart would be torn to shreds. Why, then, do we not have a problem with cheating on our King? To yield our minds, hearts, and bodies to anything but the truth as revealed in Scripture is to sleep with the enemy.

The open mind is not the answer. First of all, it's not Christianity; it's merely a self-ruled existence attempting to masquerade as sweetly and humbly religious. Historic Christianity is first and foremost Christ-ruled and it has always esteemed the value not of an *open mind*, but of a *canon-mind*. Allow me to explain.

The canon-mind is the most honest, happy, holy, and healthy mind in the universe. It's a mind controlled by the person of Jesus Christ, esteeming the things that He esteems, despising the things He despises. It is a mind in tune with Heaven, discriminating between light and darkness with the deftness of God Himself. It is a mind radically loyal to the words of Scripture, unbending to opposition, unyielding to doubt, and unwavering in its allegiance. The canon-mind discerns friend from foe, it recognizes lie from truth, and it will give its life to preserve the distinction.

The idea of the canon-mind can only be understood through understanding the idea of canon itself (which, by the way, is not a Civil War piece of artillery that shoots lead balls). So let's take a little bit of time to fully wrap our minds around the extraordinary idea of canon.

What Is Canon?

The concept of canon is one of my favorite themes in Scripture. In fact, if I can convince Leslie to consider it for the future (which has proven a difficult thing in the past), I think it would be a great boy's name. It is a name jammed full of grit, strength, and manly authority.

Ironically, the word *canon* isn't found in Scripture, although the idea is replete throughout the 66 books. The word is derived from the Hebrew word for *rod*, which is another word for *branch* or *reed*. And if you are a student of Scripture, the words *rod, branch,* and *reed* are very familiar.

The idea of a rod, in Scripture, is very important for understanding the idea of canon. A rod (a branch of a tree cut, carved, and finished) is a very familiar component of the Hebrew culture and basically has four uses, as described in the Bible:

1. It was a tool for measurement (a measuring stick)[1]
2. It was a tool for discipline and correction[2]

3. Shepherds used a rod to gently guide, comfort, and enable their sheep[3]

4. Kings held a rod in their right hand as their symbol for authority and ruling power[4]

If you examine those four things closely, you will notice that the purpose of a rod is the precise purpose of the Bible, which has historically been defined as the canon of God:

1. The Bible is God's measuring stick for our lives. It is the perfect measurement of righteousness that proves each and every one of us to have failed in our measurement against heavenly perfection. It also describes the perfect measurements of the heavenly temple and the perfect measurements of the Messiah soon to come (which were both fulfilled in the person of Jesus Christ) in order that when He came to Earth, He would be recognized.

2. The Bible is God's tool to awaken us to error and correct our souls. As Paul says in the second book of Timothy, "All Scripture is profitable for reproof and correction."[5]

3. The Bible also is God's means of guiding us forward as little sheep in this dangerous, wolf-infested world. It is "for instruction in righteousness: that the man of God may be perfect, thoroughly furnished unto all good works."[6]

4. And the Bible is the word of the King, who has the power, authority, and strength to control our lives, judge our lives, and save our lives.[7]

I believe the idea of canon is one of the most critical concepts missing from a vast spectrum of the Christian church today. And as a result, the integrity *of* and confidence *in* the Word of God are at stake. For instance, there are many today who question "Why these sixty-six books?" The thought is, "Who decided to pick the book of James and exclude the Gospel of Judas?" If you don't understand the concept of canon, then the Bible appears to be an ancient collection of books deemed divine by some troupe of subjective and biased gray-headed men back in the dark ages. It seems like a humanly contrived process rather than a divine one governed by the God-principle of canon.

Let me briefly attempt to explain the principle of canon:

Throughout this world there are billions of branches from millions of trees, and out of these billions of branches somehow the "true branches" must be discerned. How can you recognize the true from the false? You will recognize the true branches because they will originate from the same root, bear likeness to the rest of the divine tree, and bear identical fruit to the rest of the "true" branches. God established a test, a "proving," if you will, to determine if something is to be determined canon. And this test is a hard one. If there be any discrepancy, any question, even the slightest variation or contradiction, then the branch will be deemed false.

The Bible can be likened to a great tree with 66 branches. But this tree didn't start with 66 branches. Every branch had to be added over time. And to be added, each branch must first have endured the supremely difficult "test of canonicity."

1. It had to prove that it came from the same root—in other words, that it was inspired by God Himself.

2. It had to bear perfect likeness to the rest of the existing branches on the tree and could not contradict or bear the nature of a different type of tree. It had to align to perfection without a single fault.

3. And it had to evidence fruit identical to the fruit on the rest of the existing branches, showcasing in its life the exact same nature as the root from which it was born.

The canon has divine authority to rule and control. So whatever possesses the distinction of canon becomes...

1. a measuring rod against which all other ideas or truths must be measured, and all men must be judged, as well as all other aspiring measuring rods must be tested;

2. a correcting rod by which all men must come into alignment and all rebellion is driven from the heart of men;

3. a shepherd's rod that guides, comforts, and enables men down the narrow way of God's kingdom path;

4. and a King's rod that silences all opposing opinion, holding all

authority to define truth, righteousness, and the nature of sin, death, life, salvation, and the world to come.

So, it goes without saying that we must be careful as to what ends up being included amongst the canon of God. And it should also go without saying why this issue of canon has been at the center of the great battle for truth throughout the ages. For, as the enemy of truth knows well, if you can cast doubt on canon ("Did God really say that?"), you in effect remove its power and authority to rule and control.

This battle over canon authority started out at the very inception point of the Bible. Moses (the author of the first five books of the canon), along with his brother Aaron, the first high priest of Israel, were confronted by some of the leading men of the nation of Israel (this is known historically as the Korah Rebellion[8]). These leaders wanted to know, regarding Moses and Aaron, the very same thing most of us want to know about the Bible: "Who gave you the authority to rule over us? Who picked you to be in charge? Why is it that you are so special and what you say is deemed truth?" The questions they asked are strangely reminiscent of the questions our modern culture, including our modern church culture, ask about the Word of God.

But God had a solution for this question of authority. There were 12 tribes in Israel (ironically, in the Old Testament Hebrew text, the word *tribe* is the same word as *branch* or *rod*), and God asked Moses to direct the chief of each of these 12 tribes to inscribe their name upon their personal rods (each chief had a rod because he was the prince of his people and had authority over his house) and to bring them into the tabernacle of God. They were to leave their rods in the tabernacle overnight and, in the morning, the question of "canonicity" would be solved. God made it clear that whoever's rod budded and bore the evidence of life in the night would be shown to be the one appointed by God and the one holding the authority of God in the camp of Israel. His would be the true rod, the true branch.

Well, as the story goes, in the morning, all 12 rods were brought out from the tabernacle and laid before the people of Israel. And one rod, the rod of Aaron (the brother of Moses, the high priest of Israel), was different than the others. For overnight, it blossomed and bore almonds.

God established the canonicity of Moses and Aaron from the

beginning. He built the governmental ruling authority within the Hebrew republic on the idea of the "budded rod." In fact, this rod was so important that it was one of the three things placed in the Ark of the Covenant that sat in the Holy of Holies in the temple of God.

Moses was hallmarked by God as being authoritative and possessing the divine right to rule and control Israel, and therefore, his writings (Genesis, Exodus, Leviticus, Numbers, and Deuteronomy) were seen, by all Israel, as canon and the first measuring rod by which all other future rods (or books of the Bible) would need to be measured.

The Hebrew culture took the idea of canon very seriously. Nothing should be considered of the divine root without overwhelming evidence. Thus were the 39 books of the Old Testament built and put together over a 1000-year period of time. Every book was weighed in the light of the revealed truth of the existing canon, measured against it, tested against it, and then determined, after much scrutiny, to be inspired of God.

It's also important to note how Jesus fits into the idea of canon.

I get giddy with excitement over this idea of canon. For it is central to the credibility and authority of the person of Jesus and the entire New Testament, and therefore, Christianity. When it is realized that Jesus actually *is* canon—that He is the rod that budded before all Israel, proving Him not only the rightful authority over Israel, but also that He was Immanuel (God with us)—then the entire idea of Christianity rises to an entirely new level of esteem.

> In the beginning was the Word, and the Word was with God, and the Word was God.[9]

The entirety of the Old Testament builds a "canon test" for the Messiah. And this Messiah must measure against this existing rod, or in a greater sense, this existing tree of rods (known as the Law and the Prophets), and demonstrate to all Israel that He, in fact, is perfect, of the same root, without contradiction, bearing identical fruit, and that He fulfills everything spoken of Him.

This canon test would be impossible for a mere man to pass. Here is a very simplified overview of the main component parts to the canon test for the Messiah:

- He must prove to be the Son of God[10]

- He must prove to be of the seed of the woman[11]
- He must prove to be of the seed of Abraham[12]
- He must prove to be of the seed of Isaac[13]
- He must prove to be of the seed of David[14]
- He must be born of a virgin; He must be Immanuel, God with us[15]
- He must be born in Bethlehem, Judea[16]
- Kings must fall down before him, offering gifts[17]
- He must be called out of Egypt[18]
- Elijah must come before Him[19]
- He must be anointed with the Spirit[20]
- His ministry must commence in Galilee[21]
- He must enter Jerusalem riding upon a colt[22]
- He must be undesirable to many[23]
- He must be meek[24]
- He must be without guile[25]
- He must be consumed with zeal for God's house[26]
- He must bear reproach[27]
- He must be betrayed by a friend[28]
- When He is stricken, His sheep must be scattered[29]
- He must be sold for 30 pieces of silver, and the potter's field must be purchased with the money[30]
- He must be numbered with the criminals[31]
- He must make intercession for His murderers[32]
- He must die[33]
- His bones must not be broken[34]
- He must be pierced[35]
- Lots must be cast for His clothes[36]
- He must rise again from the dead[37]
- He must ascend[38]
- He must sit at the right hand of God[39]
- He must be both King and Priest[40]

Six different times within the Old Testament, a man known as the

"Branch" is foretold. These six references are some of the most thrilling passages in the Bible, obviously pertaining to the coming Messiah, Jesus Christ. To the Hebrew mind it is basically saying, "The True Canon" is coming, the Rod of all rods will soon appear, the Authority over all other authorities will come and blossom and bear almonds in your midst. In Zechariah chapter 3 we read, "Behold, I will bring forth my servant the BRANCH...and I will remove the iniquity of that land in one day" (verses 8-9). And again in Zechariah chapter 6 we read, "Behold the man whose name is The BRANCH; and he shall grow up out of his place, and he shall build the temple of the LORD: even he shall build the temple of the LORD; and he shall bear the glory, and shall sit and rule upon his throne; and he shall be a priest upon his throne: and the counsel of peace shall be between them both" (verses 12-13). Over and over again this Branch (or Canon) is described, and every time it is speaking of Jesus Christ.[41]

It is my belief that Jesus is the "Rod that budded" and that He is the Great High Priest over Israel entrusted with all authority and power to rule and control my life. I believe that He passed the test of canon with bewildering, supernaturally inspired perfection and that He has proven that He is, indeed, the canon of Scripture in bodily form, or as the apostle John put it, the Word of God become flesh:

- He is the Measuring Rod, the Perfection of Righteousness, the Fulfillment of the Law
- He is the Word of God, profitable for doctrine, for reproof, for correction, and for instruction in righteousness
- He is Grace, Comfort, and Salvation
- He is the King of kings and Lord of lords

Because Jesus passed the canon test of the Old Testament, He is the "Rod of rods" fit to measure and define the canonicity of the 27 New Testament books as well. Jesus personally and uniquely hallmarked the lives of the 12 apostles as canon-bearers. They each, including Paul, witnessed His life, death, and resurrection, and bore in their lives and speech the power and authority of the "Canon made flesh." And as a result, they were used by God to pen the final books of the great canon and fully express the remaining elements of the perfection and person of Jesus Christ.

But even the 27 books of the New Testament had to be tested and proven against the harsh standard of the existing canon. Every book in the New Testament, before it was added, had to match to the perfection of the entire Old Testament canon, just as Jesus had to.

Note: The reason the Apocrypha (the collection of books written during the 400 years of silence between the Old Testament and the New Testament) is not included in the Protestant/evangelical canon is because it can't stand up to the canon test of the Old Testament. There are many points in which the Apocrypha contradicts the first 39 books of the Bible and therefore was never received by the Jewish people as canon. The apocryphal writings are insightful works, full of fascinating ideas and laden with truths, but they aren't canon, and they shouldn't be given the position of authority and rulership in our lives that the rest of the Bible possesses.

Another note: This issue of canon brings up a significant variance between Protestant/evangelical Christianity and Catholicism. The Catholic Church includes the Apocrypha in its definition of canon because the Catholic Church does not use the same canon test that the Hebrews and the Protestant/evangelical church utilize. Since Pope Paul III and the Council of Trent almost 500 years ago declared the Apocrypha to be canon, it was considered canon. In the Catholic Church, the Pope is canon, and therefore the definer of truth and righteousness, whereas in the Hebrew system of thought and the Protestant/evangelical system of thought, it is Scripture that is the final arbiter of truth and righteousness.

Even yet *another* note: This new narrative way of thinking that Brian McLaren, Rob Bell, and the rest of the emergent establishment are presenting goes one step further even than Catholicism, making each and every one of us popes. In fact, emergent thinking is popery on steroids. It's saying, in effect, "We, the modern community of believers determine, by democratic process, what truth is, even if it violates Scripture, we have final authority" (see, for example, Rob Bell's statements on page 172). Where is the fear of God? We all should stay at a safe distance from these fellows for fear that lightning will strike at any moment.

Okay, back to the book:

As I mentioned earlier, the matter of canon is one of my favorite ideas in Scripture. It demonstrates the brilliance of God, the majesty of His

Word, and the sacred nature of the 66 canon-tested books within the Bible. But my favorite thought is that Jesus Himself is canon. He is the One who created the entire Hebrew culture, inspired all the 39 books leading up to His birth, made the canon-test for His existence literally impossible for a mere man to pass, and then blossomed and bore almonds before the entire nation of Israel, proving Himself the fulfillment of it all. He is the canon made flesh.

So what is the canon-mind?

A canon-mind is the ancient Judeo-Christian way of thinking and reasoning. It is a mind fashioned after the brilliance of the 66 canon-tested-and-proven books of the Bible. It is a mind that is simply intolerant of any mind-set, worldview, or outlook that contradicts or challenges the substance of this budded rod known as Scripture.

If a thought or idea doesn't pass the three tests of canon, then it simply has no business being entertained. After all, why would we want to lug around inside our minds anything that is hostile and contrary to the King of the universe?

1. Every mind-set, worldview, and the ideas contained within them have to prove that they originate from the same root as Scripture did, which is God Himself. It has to be completely congruent, without even a shadow of difference, without even the slightest hint of contradiction.

2. Every mind-set, worldview, and the ideas contained within them have to bear perfect likeness to all 66 branches (or books) on the canon tree (the Bible). They have to be completely congruent, without even a shadow of difference, without even the slightest hint of contradiction.

3. Every mind-set, worldview, and the ideas contained within them have to evidence identical fruit to the fruit described in the 66 canon-tested books. They must bear the marks of love, joy, peace, holiness, victory, and hostility toward the kingdom of darkness, and so on (this list is a rather long one). But, long and short, every mind-set, worldview, and the ideas contained within them must showcase in its life the exact same nature as the root from which it was born.

So what if the mind-set, worldview, or the ideas contained within them don't match up? What should we do then? In the book of 2 Corinthians, we are told to bring "into captivity every thought" (10:5). We can't let our thoughts run free, painting its graffiti on the walls of our mind. We must give contrary thought no room to maneuver in our life. In Romans 16:17, Paul says that we should "mark" those things that don't align and "avoid them."

The canon-mind *is* an open mind, but it is a mind open *only* to the thoughts, ideas, patterns, and ways of God.

The canon-mind *is* a prejudiced mind (I happily admit it), but it is a mind prejudiced against anything and everything that would dare diminish the preeminence of the living God.

The open mind masquerades as a more loving mind-set, as a more accepting and more humble and honest mind-set. But it is a mind that completely overlooks the fact that we are in the midst of hostile territory, that there are two kingdoms at war, and that the number one device of the enemy kingdom is to warp and pollute truth with the poison of error as well as the minds of all those who ingest such a damnable concoction.

Like I said earlier, the canon-mind is the most honest, happy, holy, and healthy mind in the universe. It's a mind controlled by the person of Jesus Christ, esteeming the things that He esteems, despising the things He despises. It is a mind in tune with Heaven, discriminating between light and darkness with the deftness of God Himself. It is a mind radically loyal to the words of Scripture, unbending to opposition, unyielding to doubt, and unwavering in its allegiance. The canon-mind discerns friend from foe, it recognizes lie from truth, and it will give its life to preserve the distinction.

It's shocking to me that anyone could suggest that any other form of a mind might bring glory and pleasure to our King of kings. Our Lord Jesus esteems faithfulness and loyalty, and the canon-mind is our way of loving Him with every thought entertained within our being. It's our way of knocking the enemy in the teeth when he comes to the door of our mind, our homes, and our churches, and saying, "Over my dead body! This is my King's house! Now get out of here!"

Part Six

The Artful Dodger

Playing Johnnie Cochran with God

Twenty-four

MIRANDA

Sixteen years ago I sat sweating in the third row of a crowded gymnasium-turned-sanctuary. My head was bent down and plastered against my pleading palms. I was awaiting the introduction, and my stomach was churning with tension.

"Now, we are going to hear from a young man from Denver, Colorado." The guy introducing me was reading from a card, and not very effectively. He looked toward the side of the stage and asked, "Is his name Derrick or Darren?"

"Derrick!" came the incorrect answer from the people in the know.

"Derrick Woody is preparing to head over to Belgium…"

"Bulgaria!" came the correction from the right side of the stage. This time at least it was accurate.

"I'm sorry, Bulgaria, in a couple weeks to share the gospel." Again the man lost his spot on the card and spent, what felt like a minute, trying to find his place. "He is here with his missionary team and is going to be talking to us about purity. Please welcome…" the man studied the note card once more to find my name, "Darren Ludy!"

Now, let me give you a little background on this nerve-racking, awkward speaking opportunity.

There were about 25 of us on this missionary team, and we were traveling the United States for a month doing gigs in churches, offering humanitarian aid wherever we went, and basically attempting to bring the gospel to as many people as we could possibly reach in 31 days. Then it was off to Eastern Europe to change the world. This was supposed to be a grand adventure, but we spent most of our time stuck on the side of the road and in automotive repair shops due to the rickety nature of our bus. Who knows how many hungry mechanics' children went to bed with bellies full thanks to that intermittent bus?

Well, the whole awkward speaking thing started one afternoon while we were chugging down the Louisiana interstate. The topic of purity came up in the bus. It was a localized conversation, basically contained to the middle five rows. The question was, How far is too far? And, I accidentally shocked everyone with my answer. They simply couldn't believe me when I said that I loved my wife even though I hadn't yet met her, was writing her love letters and love songs even then, and was actually considering the idea of not even kissing her until our wedding day. In hindsight, I probably should have held back a little and let them just chew on the "I love my future wife even now" concept. But long and short, I said it, it stuck, it got passed around, and there was a general hubbub amidst my 25 colleagues.

When we arrived in Monroe, Louisiana, the stage was set. We were attending a community-wide youth rally in some large church, and were going to put on one of our skits for the crowd. But the leaders of the youth rally were in need of a speaker. In fact, they were hoping someone on our missionary team could talk to everyone about purity. Well, our leader had heard some rumor floating around that Eric Ludy had a lot to say on the subject and whammo—he said, "I've got just the guy for the job!"

My leader didn't give me a lot of options regarding the topic. Purity it was, and in 15 minutes nonetheless. And, to my dismay, there were at least 500 kids clamoring about inside this sweltering gymnasium.

So I sat there with my head bent down, buried in my up-facing palms. The poor introduction was distracting, but the tension I felt was due to a fierce "God-induced" pressure upon my heart and not merely due to the self-defending grief over the fact that this man butchered my name twice in less than 45 seconds.

That moment in Monroe, Louisiana, mere seconds before I walked up onto the stage, marks one of the most significant moments of my young life. I was given only 15 minutes to prepare, but strangely I already knew what I was supposed to say. And I didn't want to say it. I knew what God was asking me to speak. And I didn't want to speak it.

I had recently told God, "Whatever You ask, I will do!" And yet here

I was wrestling with the age-old battle of the soul: to seek applause from men or from God, to seek to be cool or to seek to be a Christian.

"God, please don't ask me to say that. Please! Please!"

My stomach was knotted up in a ball and my heart was thumping chaotically within my chest.

"God...I'm willing," I gasped inwardly as the clock ticked down to zero. And it was then that I made the pact with the Almighty. "Even if I am rejected, laughed off the stage, told to leave, ridiculed and scorned, I will do it. I will do it for You!"

As I write this, that was 16 years ago, almost to the day. And still today I am defined by my decision to speak the unpopular thing that night. It is almost as if you can look at my life and follow the trajectory that was set in motion that night, and it would lead to the very point I am at right now in life.

I spoke for only about ten minutes. I literally trembled as I talked, the microphone quaking in my grip. My voice evidenced my discomfort, and when I was done, I nearly fainted with exhaustion. The entire time I spoke, the gymnasium was silent. No one moved, no one coughed, no one itched, no one laughed, no one seemed to breathe. There were no "Amens," no proclamations of "Preach it, brother!" And I was met with stony silence as I concluded. There was no applause, no encouraging backslapping as I left the stage. I was greeted only by harshness, coldness, and a shiver of disgust.

The man who had preceded me chuckled awkwardly as he meandered back onto the stage. He looked out over the frozen audience and said good-humoredly, "Don't worry, I'm not here to preach holiness!"

That scene ranks up there as one of the most awkward I've ever endured. And there was a piece of me that never wanted to find myself in such a miserable situation ever again.

Even though no one had bothered to stick me in the back of a squad car and read me my Miranda rights, I most certainly learned the hard way that anything you say in defense of holiness, righteousness, and purity can and will be used against you in a court of law.

All I did was speak a little manly stuff. And you would have thought that I had just squashed a puppy dog up on stage. What did I say? Well, I told everyone that, first and foremost, Jesus didn't come to earth to get for Himself a merely *abstinent* bride. And that His great and eternal goal in our life wasn't just physical virginity. In fact, above anything, our God is after *spiritual* virginity—purity in the innermost recesses of our hearts and minds. I basically said, "If there is anything in your heart and mind that is opposite of God's nature, then it needs to go, pure and simple!"

Manly stuff might be true stuff, but it comes across to the soul like a paintball thwacking the side of the head.

About an hour after the youth rally was over, three of the team's leaders approached me in private.

"Eric," one said, "we feel you owe the team an apology."

"You basically stood up there on stage, representing all of us, and brought condemnation!" said another.

Then the third one added, "We have enough problems with legalism nowadays. We don't need to be contributing to the problem!"

They were very upset. I was still reeling from the whole affair anyway, so to now add this extra spanking to my already-sore spiritual backside was a lot for my 20-year-old inner man to handle.

Why is it that quite often the only person who gets rebuked, confronted, or called out in metrotheistic Christianity is not the sinner, but the one taking a stand against the sin?

I didn't feel that I should apologize for speaking something that, in the first place, was truth, and in the second place, was something God was nudging me to speak. I didn't speak with a dour tone, a harsh edge, or an angry attitude. I spoke with humility, gentleness, and love. It wasn't my intent to stir people up. I honestly hoped that they would come to understand what I was saying, because it had personally transformed my life.

As uncomfortable as this whole affair was for my 20-year-old soul, I can honestly say now that the whole situation was strangely beneficial, at least for me.

To be accused of bringing condemnation is a horrible thing. Bringing condemnation is one of the most terrible "hate crimes" any Christian could possibly commit. Is that what I was doing up there on stage?

And to also be accused of legalism, if it isn't worse, at least ranks right up there with bringing condemnation on the list of Christian no-no's. Was I propagating legalism while I spoke?

When you are 20, you don't always know how to respond to your critics in a way that sounds polished and intelligent. I don't know what I said back then to my detractors, but I'm sure it wasn't very impressive.

On the other hand, one of the greatest revivalists of yesteryear once responded to similar criticism by saying, "If the church were half as afraid of sin as it is of legalism then she would be a perfect and holy bride without spot or wrinkle."[1]

I've come to find out that when you bring the manly stuff, the Christian community is trained, like Pavlov's dog, to start screaming the words, "That's judgmental!" or "That's condemning!" or "That's legalism!" The manly stuff is a lot of things, but it is absolutely, without equivocation none of the above-mentioned hate crimes.

The manly stuff often causes something inside of us to revolt. It seems to poke at our pride, our comforts, and our cultural sensibilities. When the manly stuff comes thundering into our lives, it exposes the fact that we are rebellious and that we prefer to hold the control position in our lives and that we aren't, in truth, interested in turning those controls over to Jesus Christ anytime soon.

The manly stuff is the stuff of revolutionaries. It nails letters to Wittenberg doors, it speaks that one thing that needs to be spoken, it is the hard stuff of the gospel that makes certain that the Christian life is healthy and on course.

I can fully understand why many of us don't like it. But let's get something straight: Even though the manly stuff may not allow us to comfortably sit back and stay in our cozy insulated little world, and even though it may convict of sin and call us on to a life of faith and righteousness, the manly stuff is not judgmental, condemning, or legalistic. In fact, the manly stuff is often kept at bay from entering back into the modern church due to this massive misunderstanding.

Twenty-five

A FACE WITHOUT EYES, A FACE WITHOUT TEARS

Ten months ago I realized that I live in Suburbia, USA. I realize that this is something that should have proven quite obvious to me long before, but I simply didn't think about it. I've spent 36 years in Suburbia, and so Suburbia is just "what life is" to me. It's known, it's comfortable, it's predictable, it's safe.

It's very easy to become insulated from the real world when living in Suburbia. In fact, the reason Suburbia even exists is for the purposes of insulation. After all, if you had an option between living amidst a den of drug lords, pimps, and gang violence or separate from it all in Beaver Cleaver Village, who in their right mind wouldn't choose Beaver Cleaver Village?

I've chosen Beaver Cleaver Village my entire life. But one thing God has pressed into my soul as of late is that the heart and soul of the Bravehearted Gospel demands me to get outside this cozy village. It's pushing me where the destitution, the enslavement, the prostitution, and the street children are. The bravehearted life is a life lived where Jesus lived—a life spent on the same things Jesus spent His life on.

I'll admit it up front. This is an uncomfortable thought for me. I have a particular fondness for the lack of destitution, enslavement, prostitution, and street children in Suburbia, USA. And to be honest, I would rather throw prayers and money in the general direction of the problem instead of getting my family intertwined in the whole mess. Keeping a healthy distance from all this sinful disease just seems to be a wiser course of action. I've always promised God that if I see someone naked I will certainly clothe him, or if I see someone hungry, I will feed him, or if I see someone in prison, I will visit him. But fortunately for me, I live in Disneyland. There are no street children to be found in the magic kingdom, especially not in the vicinity of Cinderella's enchanted castle. And of course, all the starving, naked people have, thankfully, been briskly escorted to the nearest exit. So, the odds are pretty much slim to next to none that I will ever be put in the supremely uncomfortable position of even having to see one of these unsightly people, much less keep my promise to feed, clothe, and care for them.

I have often heard it said that justice is blind. But now that I think of it, so is ignorance.

I've found that, in so many areas, I think and reason like a suburban American Christian. I can rationalize with the best of them as to why suburban dwellers are just as important as "the least of these." After all, suburban dwellers need Jesus, too! It's not their fault that they live in Suburbia! If we take the gospel to the lost and the least around the world, then aren't we basically abandoning our friends and family back home?

That's simply not bravehearted thinking. That's self-protective reasoning. In fact, it has been proven true throughout the ages that when the church abandons itself for the least around the world, the church and the lost "back home" are awakened. The suburban church needs something more than Bible studies, homiletically groomed sermons, and Wednesday night prayer sessions to move us out of our lethargy. We need a life-and-death adventure—something to wake up for in the morning that infuses spiritual caffeine into the bloodstream. We need a Someone to die for and a version of living that is wholly and altogether supernaturally enabled. The lost aren't being awakened by our self-indulgent lives; and they aren't being drawn to Jesus by our flickering lamps of religion. What the perishing world needs is to see the body of Jesus Christ actually living out the gospel. They need to see the love, power, and passion of God, down here on earth, in flesh and blood, once again! As Ravenhill says, "A blazing bush drew Moses; a blazing church will attract the world, so that from its midst they will hear the voice of the living God."[1] Now that's what I call beauty and allure! The beauty of Heaven and the allure of the Spirit as He draws dead and dying men and women into the arms of their redeeming Savior!

Leonard Ravenhill put it another way. He said, "What is your life? It

is even a vapor that appeareth for a little time and then vanisheth away...
That world outside there is not waiting for a new definition of Christianity, it's waiting for a new demonstration of Christianity."[2]

When the manly stuff challenges us in this arena of lifestyle we have a tendency to get defensive, even mad. I have no qualms with Christians living in Suburbia, but I feel that if we do, we must adopt a lifestyle, while living in Suburbia, that seeks and saves the lost, and rescues those considered the least among society. Suburbia must not prove our spiritual undoing. Otherwise, it must be dragged to the dump along with all the rest of the trash.

The spirit of the Bravehearted Gospel demands that the Christian life be *spent* and not *preserved*. It says with Paul, "To live is Christ, and to die is gain!"[3] In fact, one of the best ways to enunciate the aims of the gospel in our lives is to be made strong, made whole, and made able in order that we might be poured out for those who are weak, broken, and paralyzed. This is the pattern of Christ.

Suburbia is often an insulation—an unconscious protective coating that hinders us from ever seeing, hearing, or experiencing the call of God upon our lives. We may be willing to clothe the naked, but we never see them; and never seeing them, our hearts never break, and our eyes never weep. We may be willing to feed the hungry, but the hungry aren't going to be knocking on the doors of our suburban communities any time soon. We may even be enthusiastic about helping orphans, but unless we actually seek them out, we'll never be able to "save" them.

Jesus left Suburbia.

He left Heaven, He left comfort and beauty, He left splendor and glory, He left power, He left riches and fame and a thousand untold splendors besides—all to come down and dwell in this squalid, sin-ridden, darkened world of hate and spite.

Why?

Because He is the Great Shepherd and He came to seek and to save that which was lost!

He came for the destitute, the enslaved, the prostituted, the addicted, and the diseased. He came for the naked, the lonely, the suicidal, the broken, and the battered. He came for you. He came for me. He took on flesh and He dwelt among us. And He was not untouched by our infirmities.

And how can we, His body, who have received both His grace and His commission to be His ambassadors to the world, how can we remain untouched by the infirmities of our fellow man? How, when the Lord of Glory, the Almighty, poured out His strength so that the weak could become strong? How can we justify hoarding our strength and ignoring the weak?

If we are truly the body of Christ with hands and feet numbering in the millions, then why aren't we serving the same needy outcasts that Jesus Himself served, when His hands and feet only numbered two?

Now if you're feeling a bit uncomfortable with this chapter, I don't blame you. This whole section is neck deep in the manly stuff, and we're not used to being exposed to it at all. That's because this protective, suburban coating affects far more than just what sort of people we meet during our average day. It also affects how we think. We, as the modern church, have created a "Suburbia of Doctrine" that functions sort of like a gated community around our hearts and minds. It's a very posh, Beaver Cleaver Village within our souls, armed with 24-hour security guards hired to keep the manly stuff of the gospel at arm's length.

Twenty-six

The New Legalism

We, the suburban American church, have unconsciously crafted a rather intricate protective gate about our Christian Beaver Cleaver Village life. We like our comforts, we like our addictions to sports, we like our movie fetishes, we like parading our finest features on MySpace, we like our materialistic ways, we like our gluttonous consumption, we like rating our top 100 beers, of course, all in the context of "expressing our Christian liberty"!

Meanwhile, an entire world is dying while we go about our carefree existence leaving the problems of human trafficking and child prostitution to God. Do we not realize that God's problems are by their very nature, *our problems?* Do we not realize that we are *His body?* We are His hands to serve the least, we are His might to swing His sword, we are His army to crush the jaws of the wicked and to rescue the dying from their fangs. We are His feet to leap the high wall, rush into the fray, engage the oppressor, and dart for safety with His treasure in our grip. We are His mouth to command the forces of Hell to fall back in obeisance, to preach the words of hope to the masses, and to proclaim the year of the Lord's favor. Christ is in the business of building a church that will perfectly bring the heart of God, the passion of God, and the power of God to bear upon all that is considered a *problem* to God—a church that will give no quarter to sin, to the flesh, or to the oppressors of the weak!

"But, that's legalism!" I can already hear the complaint.

The suburban church has come up with three very specific charges that are constantly brought against the manly stuff of the gospel, barring it from entry into the minds and souls of believers. The first and most famous is, of course, "That's legalism!" The other two are just as familiar to all of us modern Christians: "That's condemning" and "That's judgmental."

Now, let's define these phrases not in accordance with the Bible, but in accordance with what our modern suburban Christian world assumes them to mean.

That's Legalism—anything of a higher standard that makes me feel like I'm not where I should be in my Christian life. Anything that suggests that I must *do* something in order to be right with God, because a true Christian isn't supposed to ever *do* anything, he is only supposed to *be*. Example: "Don't talk to me about praying more—that's legalism! Don't say that I need to change—that's legalism!"

That's Condemning—anything that makes me feel uncomfortable in my soul and makes me recognize my sin. Anything that makes me squirm under the weight of conviction, because God doesn't want me to feel bad about myself, He wants me to be filled with confidence and self-esteem. Example: "You can't say that my behavior is selfish—that's condemning! Who are you to proclaim that my addiction to pornography is a sin? That's condemning!"

That's Judgmental—anything that makes it sound as if you have found something that I haven't yet discovered. Anything that comes across to me as overly confident and kind of seems like you are declaring that the way you see things is the only way—because everyone knows no one can be right about anything definitively; everyone is just guessing. Example: "Are you telling me that unless I actually yield my life over to Jesus, I can't call myself a Christian? Well, that's judgmental! Are you saying that Jesus was actually born of a virgin and that you think I'm off base simply because I don't believe it? Well, that's judgmental!"

It's hard for me to imagine that if you have grown up in or around the modern church system that you haven't already been introduced to these heavy-duty "suburban insulation" devices. If ever a standard is raised it can be shot down as legalism; if ever a message crosses the line and starts to bring about the heat of conviction then it can be rationalized away as false due to the fact that it was condemning; and if ever someone brings forth the truth of Heaven straight out of the Bible without any qualifiers in full concentration with passion and ardor it is immediately discounted as judgmental.

How is the manly stuff supposed to enter back into the church with this massive fortified community gate standing in the way? Well, that's the whole point of the gate, isn't it—to keep this gritty and uncomfortable stuff out? Deep down, we really want to be insulated from all this manly stuff. We don't want to face the facts that the Christian life isn't about me, about my wants, about meeting my desires, or about stroking my flesh. It's about Jesus Christ and a radical abandon to His wants, His desires, and adoring the love and power found only in His name.

Joseph Parker said, "The man whose little sermon is 'repent' sets himself against his age, and will for the time being be battered mercilessly by the age of whose moral tone he challenges. There is but one end for such a man—'off with his head!' You had better not preach repentance until you have pledged your head to heaven."[1]

As suburbanite Christians, we have constructed a self-protecting gate about our souls, and as a result we are starving of truth, absent of power, and wholly devoid of victory. We need a man's sword, a man's muscle, and a man's passion to enter into our hearts once again. We need the manly stuff. And let me assure you, this manly stuff is not in even the remotest way legalistic, condemning, or judgmental, but rather energizing, life-giving, and stoked with the flame of faith.

These heavy-duty insulation devices that we have unwittingly concocted in the church simply have to go! They are both a form of gross ignorance as well as gross selfishness. I am the first one to say if something is genuinely legalistic, condemning, or judgmental that we should drive it out of the church with a crushing blow to the teeth. However, when we redefine these words to fit our personal self-protective agenda, and thus keep the true spiritual muscle outside of our lives, we are in grave danger of being swallowed up by the enemy of our souls.

I hate legalism as much as probably many of you do. But the legalism of which I'm speaking is quite different than the trumped-up idea that many in our culture today have of it. The basic characteristic of legalism is attempting to do in our own strength that which only God can do, or as I always like to say, "Self's attempt at imitating God's perfection." Whenever someone brings a message that basically says, "*You* can do it!"

that is the essence of legalism. But when someone brings the message, "*God* can do it!" that is the essence of biblical Christianity.

We have become so paranoid these days of "doing" anything that we've become obese felines lounging on our spiritual couches. But our God is a lover of action. In fact, He detests lethargy and slothfulness. And when we yield our bodies to Him, He moves us to action. He loves *through* us, He prays *through* us, He becomes a father to the orphan *through* us, He rescues the oppressed *through* us, and He demonstrates His holiness *through* us. It is not *us* that pull off this miracle, but Christ working *in us*. "*God* can do it!" That is just Christianity 101.

Condemnation is a result of rebellion, and one is saved from condemnation by hearing truth and yielding to it. Suburban Christians get condemnation and conviction mixed up all the time. In fact, I honestly feel like most Christians believe the two are the same thing. When you feel the sting of God upon your conscience, that is conviction, *not* condemnation. When a Spirit-born message makes you squirm and your soul is sweating under the intense warmth of God's white hot searchlight, that is conviction, *not* condemnation. Conviction is always present when the Spirit of God comes. There is always discomfort, always a squirm within the soul, and always an uncomfortable heat that is laboring to expose an inner rebellion. But such discomfort is given, ironically, in order to save us *from* condemnation, not *bring* condemnation. This uncomfortable heat is brought in order to rescue us, bring us hope, and give us life abundant. Again, this is just Christianity 101.

So then what about this whole judgmental thing? I mentioned in the very beginning of this book that a manly tone of voice is deemed socially inappropriate nowadays, especially in the church. Ironically, in business, sports, action movies, military life, and in the political realm, a manly voice is still somewhat accepted. But in the arena of truth it has been exorcised as if it were a meddlesome demon. The manly voice serves up truth a bit louder, more confidently, and more passionately than we tend to prefer. But for all our cultured sensitivities, the manly voice is God's chosen means for delivering the message of truth unto His people. This is the way Moses, Joshua, and Samuel spoke, as well as David, Josiah, and Daniel. It is the way Nehemiah, Elijah, Elisha, Ezekiel, and Jeremiah spoke. It is the way John the Baptist, Jesus, Peter, and

Paul spoke. It's the way Athanasius and Luther spoke, as well as Knox, Wycliffe, Tyndale, and Bunyan. It is the voice of Zwingli, Whitefield, Wesley, Spurgeon, Tozer, and Ravenhill, and ironically, this is how the Word of God speaks right now on every page, if we would only have the eyes to see it and the ears to hear it.

Down here on earth, we may prefer the sound of the violin to the gritty sound of the prophet-preacher, but in Heaven it's totally the other way around. There is only one thing sweeter in God's ears than the manly voice of truth trumpeting the glory of God Jehovah for the peoples of this earth to hear, and that is the people of the earth responding to that voice and to that message in brokenness and repentance, calling out to God for deliverance and salvation. To Heaven's ear, there can be no sweeter sound.

There are no more excuses for us Christians. We must face the reality of what Christianity was, what it is, and what it will always be—*a call to serve and to obey our King.* The three great excuses, "That's legalism," "That's condemning," and "That's judgmental," have been used to ward off practical, real-world obedience to our Lord for years, and it's time that we admit it.

These three excuses represent a new type of "Johnnie Cochran Legalism" that has crept into the church. It's not a legalism that *prosecutes* its clients, condemning them and sentencing them under the crushing weight of the law. Rather, it is a legalism that plays the clever lawyer with God and the Bible, working the loopholes and technicalities of the law to *acquit* its clients and get them off the hook.

"Well, technically, your honor," says the New Legalism, "the law does say in Romans 4 subsection 6 that my client's righteousness, and therefore his good standing in this court, does not require works of *any* kind. We, therefore, move that all charges of drunkenness, lust, adultery, lying, hatred, bitterness, and jealousy be dismissed as well as all acts of community service as proposed by the prosecuting attorney such as Bible reading, prayer, giving to the poor, caring for widows and orphans, as well as the wholly unloving and unlawful requirement to live a just and holy life. We find all of the above charges and requirements to be wholly inconsistent with Romans 4 subsection 6 and find them to be unnecessarily restrictive, and in complete and total violation of my client's Christian liberties. Therefore my client, having endured untold oppression, harassment, and undue censure from his fundamentalist accusers now seeks the refuge of the *letter* of the law and renders a plea of not guilty."

Ah, you've got to hand it to Johnnie. He was good.

But it doesn't really matter how many earthly courts have the wool pulled over their eyes—not a single one of Johnnie's guilty clients will go unpunished. The Judge of all the Earth will do right. The judgment bar of Heaven will not be prostituted by slick attorneys and cheap arguments. Isaiah said that in the day of judgment God will sweep away the refuge of lies so that all who have made lies their refuge will stand naked before the One who *is* the Truth and who *is* the Light! God will not be fooled by legal loopholes extracted from the letter of the law that blatantly deny the spirit and overall testimony of Scripture. For, unlike the jurors in a Johnnie Cochran trial, God will not be mocked, and whatsoever a man sows, that shall he also reap.

This is not some newfangled way of teaching the law. But it *is* exactly what Paul, the apostle of *grace*, told the early church when they asked, "Are we free to sin now that we are not under the law but under grace?" His answer was brief and blunt: "God forbid!" And to the church at Corinth he said:

> Know ye not that the unrighteous shall not inherit the kingdom of God? *Be not deceived;* neither fornicators, nor idolaters, nor adulterers, nor the effeminate, nor abusers of themselves with mankind, nor thieves, nor coveters, nor drunkards, nor revilers, nor extortioners, shall inherit the kingdom of God.[2]

Be not deceived: Faith without works is dead.[3] And we can no longer afford to keep the manly emphasis on conquering and achieving practical, real-world goals at bay under the false claim of "That's legalism!" We can no longer impugn the gritty conviction of the gospel and the manly stuff's emphasis on holiness and righteousness under the banner of "That's condemning!" And we can no longer silence the voice of truth and dismiss the masculine emphasis on the just need to wage war for the right and uproot the wrong under the pretense of "That's judgmental!" We must remove this absurd insulation that we have built up about our souls. We must become vulnerable to the truth of God and allow it to pierce us deeply and break us completely, in order that it might fill us fully and alter us wholly—to God's glory and to the furtherance of His kingdom!

THE BRAVEHEARTED PATH

SOLI DEO GLORIA

Materials needed for this section:

- a clothespin
- and a brown paper bag

To better acquaint you with this bravehearted version of living, I would first like to introduce you to someone known as Old Eric. But before I do, place the clothespin on your nose and hold out the brown paper bag in front of you just in case your stomach starts to churn a bit. Maybe it's just me, but this Old Eric guy turns my stomach.

Old Eric's favorite quote: "Me, me, me, me!" I'm not sure if he ever realized that this wasn't actually a quote, but more a vocal warm-up exercise. But nonetheless, he quoted it a lot.

Old Eric's life motto: "Act as if you are the center of the universe, and maybe one day it will come true."

It's odd, but this Old Eric guy looked quite similar to me—possibly with a little less gray in his hair and a little more tone to his physique, but all in all sort of a spittin' image of yours truly. I've had a lot of friends from high school and college confuse me for the guy, but I plead ignorant of any connection to the varmint. He was a fairly likeable character, but he had this fetish for this thing called self. And as a result he was only capable of viewing everything in life in such a way as to see how he might gain advantage from it.

You will notice that I am talking about the Old Eric in past tense. This is due to the fact that he is no longer alive—he passed away a few years back, and I say, "Good riddance!" I know that sounds harsh, but if you yourself had an "evil clone" roaming the earth that had it in for you, you too might breathe a sigh of relief if he ever packed up and moved off to the netherworld.

Well, Old Eric was a player. He always knew the right things to say. He knew how to gain the attentions of a crowd, how to crack a joke that might cause people to think, *This Old Eric guy is quite hilarious!* Old Eric was a master at being liked. He loved the good opinion of a crowd, he loved to overhear the whispers amongst the throng that reinforced the fact that he was liked, accepted, and generally thought to be a classy fellow.

It's very possible had you been introduced to the Old Eric while he was still alive that you might have liked him. He smiled a lot, was very friendly, and if you were ever down he considered it his duty to cheer you up. Like I said, Old Eric was a fairly likeable character. But this whole "self fetish" thing eventually began to catch up with him. And one day in early February 1990, all the dirt came out on Old Eric.

- Come to find out, Old Eric had an ego with more electoral votes than Texas
- He didn't really care about anyone else in the whole world but himself
- All he thought about in his quiet time was how he could better his own life
- Old Eric viewed God as someone to help him reach his own personal goals
- And if Old Eric didn't get his way, he gorged himself on a massive serving of self-pity and wouldn't remove the fork from his mouth until something once again turned in his favor
- Oh, and Old Eric, for all his supposed friendliness, spent hardly a moment of his life thinking about how he could help someone less fortunate than himself

Old Eric was a putz. He was a showman, an ovation-gatherer, a fake. He had not a scrap of real substance within his soul, and he labored long and hard to hide that awful fact. Old Eric was built after the blueprint of selfishness (aka sin) and not the blueprint of the Bravehearted Gospel.

Okay, if you trust me, it is now safe to remove the clothespin and set down the brown paper bag. I introduced you to the depressing life of Old Eric merely so that the engraced life of New Eric would stand out in contrast. Yes, it's true that the New Eric might, on the outside, still look a lot like the Old version, but on the inside there has been a complete renovation.

This New Eric is being constructed according to a completely different blueprint than the Old Eric was manufactured after, and as a result, a completely different kind of human being is emerging through Eric Ludy's 37 year-old skin. It's a version of the human life that is bigger, bolder, and a bit more bombastic in its attitude and approach to daily living. There is more life, love, and laughter. And though it is merely the infantile expression of it, this New Eric is evidencing a very rough-hewn rendition of the bravehearted life. Of course, when you fully grasp how spectacular and grandiose the fully matured bravehearted life is, then you will surely chuckle when you stand my pitiful little version up next to it in contrast, but still, in my defense, a baby version of something is still a bona fide version.

At the very inception point of this bravehearted life, there is need of a drastic and life-altering encounter with the God of the universe, in which Almighty God reaches down from Heaven and yanks the attentions of the human soul away from self and radically points them outward, thereby turning mere women and men into mighty heroes. In the bravehearted pattern, God rescues the human soul from selfishness and sets it free to spend and be spent on things far more important than "me."

Old Eric officially passed away, according to spiritual medical records, somewhere in the night on February 2, 1990. However, in my opinion, he still limped about in sort of a zombielike state for quite a few years until he once again ran into the freight train of God's grace back in October of 1999. Leslie, my wife, claims to have seen the ghost of Old Eric haunt my body every so often since, but all in all, these ghost sightings have become increasingly less and less with every passing year. In fact, Leslie hasn't mentioned the ghost of Old Eric for quite some time now.

Old Eric was all about himself.

New Eric is all about Jesus Christ and everyone around him.

The bravehearted path makes New Erics, New Leslies, New Cindys,

New Petes, New Jacks, and New Sarahs. It is the path for men and women who esteem the value of Jesus Christ over the value of themselves, and the value of God's reputation over the value of their personal reputation. The bravehearted path is heavily biased against self, and if self isn't removed from both the building and the premises of the human soul, then all construction of the bravehearted life ceases until further notice is given.

The bravehearted path is loaded with the whiskery, bassy tones of manhood. But it inspires a completely different sort of manhood than is commonly known today—a brave, servanthearted, life-expending, honorable, faithful, honest, daring, stout but tenderhearted kind of masculinity. Yet everything about this amazing path rests upon one singular decision of the soul—*to oust self.*

Old Eric is all about protecting self on the throne of the human life.

New Eric is all about establishing and keeping Jesus Christ on the throne of the human life.

If self remains in the heart of a man, or the heart of the church, then the path is denigrated into a form of godliness that possesses no power to perform. But if self is ousted and the Old Eric is booted into the netherworld, then the nuclear reactor of God's Spirit is allowed to implement this awe-inspiring stuff into the very center of my body as well as into the body of Christ.

———

My buddy Ben just bought a minivan—a boring-looking, gray one. He's been trying to dupe me into buying one, too. Ben has associated words like *never-ever-no-way-no-how-and-uh-uh* with the idea of buying a minivan since we first met over eight years ago. Ben is not a minivan sort of guy; he's more Hummer-meets-large-oversized-muddy-tires. But, still, he bought himself a gray minivan.

This whole minivan thing started up this past November when the two of us met for coffee somewhere in Denver while our wives attended a baby shower.

"I just test-drove one of those FJ Cruisers!" Ben announced.

I remember that moment well because that was one of the last "normal" statements I ever heard Ben utter. It's been ten months since that fateful statement. And since that moment, we have both been altered beyond recognition. Ben is driving a gray minivan around town and I'm staying awake at nights soothing to sleep a newly adopted orphan girl from South Korea.[1]

God has walked Ben and I through a season of radical diminishment. It's as if He came down from Heaven that day in Starbucks, pulled up a chair, and said to us, "You boys are still hogging up space in your life! Remember, this whole thing isn't about you!"

When God lessens us, it always is a very personalized process. For Ben, it happened to be in his willingness to deny his pride and humbly drive a vehicle that he had promised himself he would *never* own.

"Ben," God seemed to say with a smirk, "have you ever thought about a minivan?"

For me, it was opening up my life, my home, and my heart to an orphan.

"Eric," God echoed into my heart, "please adopt My heart. Yes, it will revolutionize your life, but please allow Me to love through you."

I realize that minivans and the adoption of one single child might seem like underwhelming demonstrations of this grand idea. But this is where it starts for each one of us—with the small steps forward. From the car we drive to the clothes we wear, to how we spend every last minute of our time, to even who should be included in our description of family, the Bravehearted Gospel demands a change in *everything*. And it's not made up in just one sacrifice. It's a lifestyle of letting go and letting God express His heart in and through our obedience.

———

When I began to allow my life to start being built around the bravehearted pattern, the first thing that became obvious is that *if* this extraordinary construction project was actually going to work, there wasn't going to be any allowance in the building project for consideration of *my* personal reputation, *my* personal comforts, *my* personal bank accounts, *my* personal accomplishments, and *my* personal leisure time. Long and short, this wasn't going to be about *me*.

So if life isn't supposed to be about me, then who is it supposed to be about?

Well, I'm glad you asked. Unfortunately, the truest answer to that question is quite a bit bigger than this little book can handle. However, due to the vast importance of the answer to that all-important question, I have labored to create a very short and concise response, which by no means does the true answer justice, but may at least temporarily satisfy your curiosity.

Question: Who is this life really supposed to be about?

I can assure you, this life is not about me, it's not about you, and it's not about anyone else out there strutting around on this great, big celestial ball. Rather, this life is all about the One who covers Himself with light as with a garment, stretched out the heavens like a curtain, laid the beams of His upper chambers in the waters, makes the clouds His chariot, and walks on the wings of the wind (Psalm 104:2-3).

Whenever I begin to consider myself as fairly important, I must remember that this whole drama is all about the One who laid the foundations of the earth so that it should not be moved forever (Psalm 104:5), the One who walked this dusty Earth in the form of man and yet never once surrendered His deity, the One whose name is above every name, and the One to whom every knee will bow and every tongue will confess that He is Lord (Philippians 2:9-11).

A pause sometime during my day is all it takes to remember that this life isn't about servicing my fancy or my fame, but is about the renown of the One known as the Son of the living God (Matthew 16:16), the firstborn of every creature (Colossians 1:15); the mighty God (Isaiah 9:6), God manifest in the flesh (1 Timothy 3:16), Emmanuel, God with us (Matthew 1:23), the Almighty, which is, and which was, and which is to come (Revelation 1:8), the creator of all things (Colossians 1:16), the beginning and the ending (Revelation 1:8), He that liveth and is alive forevermore (Revelation 1:18), the Word of God (Revelation 19:13), the Word that was made flesh (John 1:14), the sent of the Father (John 10:36), the prophet of Nazareth (Matthew 21:11), a servant (Philippians 2:7), a carpenter (Mark 6:3), a man of sorrows (Isaiah 53:3), a worm, and no man (Psalm 22:6), even the accursed of God (Deuteronomy 21:23), who humbled himself unto death, even death upon a cross (Philippians 2:8).

How dare I claim the spotlight that is due the One known as the

Savior of the world (1 John 4:14), Messiah (John 4:25), the Christ of God (Luke 9:20), a lamb without blemish and without spot (1 Peter 1:19), the lamb that was slain (Revelation 5:12), the way (John 14:6), the Good Shepherd who laid down His life (John 10:11), the Great Shepherd who was brought again from the dead (Hebrews 13:20), the Chief Shepherd who will again appear (1 Peter 5:4), the vine (John 15:5), the tree of life (Revelation 2:7), the corn of wheat (John 12:24), the bread of life (John 6:35), the light of the world (John 8:12), the strength of the children of Israel (Joel 3:12-16), a strength to the poor (Isaiah 25:4), a strength to the needy in distress (Isaiah 25:4), the rock of ages (Isaiah 26:4), the rock of my strength (Psalm 62:7), the rock of my salvation (2 Samuel 22:47), the builder (Matthew 16:18; Hebrews 3:3), the foundation (1 Corinthians 3:11), a chief cornerstone (1 Peter 2:6), the temple (Revelation 21:22).

I must tremble when I realize that I have attempted to steal the applause from the One named Faithful and True (Revelation 19:11), the truth (John 14:6), the great High Priest (Hebrews 4:14), the advocate (1 John 2:1), the surety (Hebrews 7:22), the redeemer (Isaiah 59:20), the Shiloh, the peacemaker (Genesis 49:10), the most blessed forever (Psalm 21:6), the Amen (Revelation 3:14), the Holy One and the Just (Acts 3:14), the last Adam (1 Corinthians 15:45), the resurrection (John 11:25), the head of the body, the church (Colossians 1:18), the head of all principality and power (Colossians 2:10), the captain of the host of the Lord (Joshua 5:14), the captain of salvation (Hebrews 2:10), the author and finisher of our faith (Hebrews 12:2), the Lion of the tribe of Judah (Revelation 5:5), the chiefest among ten thousand (Song of Solomon 5:10), Lord of lords (Revelation 17:14), Lord of all (Acts 10:36), Lord over all (Romans 10:12), the Prince of life (Acts 3:15), the Prince of Peace (Isaiah 9:6), the King of kings (Revelation 19:16), the One born as King of the Jews (Matthew 2:2), crucified as the King of the Jews (John 19:19), the King of saints, King of nations (Revelation 15:3), King over all the Earth (Zechariah 14:4,5,9), the King of righteousness (Hebrews 7:2), the King of peace (Hebrews 7:2), the King of glory (Psalm 24:10), the King in His beauty (Isaiah 33:17), crowned with a crown of thorns (John 19:2), crowned with glory and honor (Hebrews 2:9), crowned with a crown of pure gold (Psalm 21:3), crowned with many crowns (Revelation 19:12), the One who sits as King forever (Psalm 29:10).

All self-glory must fade, all self-applause must cease, and all self-aggrandizement must instantly halt when we awaken to the One who is fairer than the children of men (Psalm 45:2), a crown of glory and beauty (Isaiah 28:5), a stone of grace (Proverbs 17:8), a nail fastened in a sure place (Isaiah 22:23), a brother born for adversity (Proverbs 17:17), a friend who sticks closer than a brother (Proverbs 18:24), a friend who loves at all times (Proverbs 17:17).

For this precious lover of our souls was obedient (Philippians 2:8), meek, lowly (Matthew 11:29), guileless (1 Peter 2:22), tempted (Hebrews 4:15), oppressed (Isaiah 53:7), despised (Isaiah 53:3), rejected (Isaiah 53:3), betrayed (Matthew 27:3), condemned (Mark 14:64), reviled (1 Peter 2:23), scourged (John 19:1), mocked (Matthew 27:29), wounded (Isaiah 53:5), bruised (Isaiah 53:5), stricken (Isaiah 53:4), smitten (Isaiah 53:4), crucified (Matthew 27:35), and forsaken (Psalm 22:1) in order to rescue me from ruin. And through it all He was *and still is* merciful (Hebrews 2:17), faithful (Hebrews 2:17), holy, harmless (Hebrews 7:26), undefiled (Hebrews 7:26), separate (Hebrews 7:26), perfect (Hebrews 5:9), glorious (Isaiah 49:5), mighty (Isaiah 63:1), justified (1 Timothy 3:16), exalted (Acts 2:33), risen (Luke 24:6), and glorified (Acts 3:13).

Every cell within my being must cry out holy, holy, holy to this One who is my portion, my maker, my husband (Isaiah 54:5), my well-beloved (Song of Solomon 1:13), my Savior (2 Peter 3:18), my hope (1 Timothy 1:1), my brother (Mark 3:35), my helper (Hebrews 13:6), my physician (Jeremiah 8:22), my healer (Luke 9:11), my refiner (Malachi 3:3), my purifier (Malachi 3:3), my Lord, Master (John 13:13), my servant (Luke 12:37), my example (John 13:15), my teacher (John 3:2), my shepherd (Psalm 23:1), my keeper (John 17:12), my feeder (Ezekiel 34:23), my leader (Isaiah 40:11), my restorer (Psalm 23:3), my resting place (Jeremiah 50:6), my meat (John 6:55), my drink (John 6:55), my passover (1 Corinthians 5:7), my peace (Ephesians 2:14), my wisdom (1 Corinthians 1:30), my righteousness (1 Corinthians 1:30), my sanctification (1 Corinthians 1:30), my redemption (1 Corinthians 1:30), my all in all (Colossians 3:11).

Since time immemorial this grand drama of Heaven has all been about Him—the One who is the Bridegroom (Matthew 9:15; Revelation 21:9), the Rose of Sharon (Song of Solomon 2:1), the Lily of the

Valley (Song of Solomon 2:1), the great I AM, the all-powerful Jehovah God.

This life is all about Jesus Christ.

——

How can any of us dare stand in the light of such a gargantuan reality as the God of the universe? How can we even take a breath without considering the magnitude and majesty of this all-powerful King?

In my coffee shop conversation with Ben, it was *this* staggering reality that came crushing down upon our souls. It was the clear picture of *Him* that brought the tears into our eyes and the trembling awe into our hearts.

All Ben and I could say was, "Please, dear Lord, get us out of the way so that *You* might be seen! Whatever must be rectified within our lives, *do it!*"

It's not just FJ Cruisers that Ben has walked away from. I've watched him come before God and say, "Strip me clean. Strip me down until there is nothing left in me that dares to shroud Your glory!" I watched my friend bring in the homeless from off the streets, enter into the prisons to share the hope of Heaven, give up his dinner to the hungry, and stay up through the night wrestling in prayer for the lost. I've seen him weep for our imprisoned modern church, begging God to revive us once again. I've watched this man known as Ben melt away and, in his place, I've seen the emergence of a man who reminds me of my King Jesus.

A bravehearted life is all about one thing—*Jesus!* Jesus must be known, Jesus must be seen, Jesus must be praised, Jesus must be honored, and Jesus must be glorified. This is the most basic element of the bravehearted life—*a passionate disregard for self so that the person of Jesus might evidence Himself with vivid clarity through the human existence.*

Anything that dares to stroke self, esteem self, applaud self, coddle self, protect self, or direct the glory toward self instead of God is the archenemy of the bravehearted existence. And as basic and as true as this sounds, this is not how the modern church is functioning today. And there aren't many of us who bear the name *Christian* these days who are exempt from such an indictment. We are living pompous lives of self-gratification these days. And it amazes me to think that, somehow, we still have the audacity to claim that these self-indulgent lives are actually the product of the gospel of our perfectly righteous and holy God who so loved the world that He *gave.*

Dear Jesus, please have mercy on us poor sinners! We honestly don't realize what we are doing! We don't understand Your vastness, Your grandeur, Your perfection, and Your legendary fame!

Somehow, somewhere along the line, we got conned into the idea that the Christian life is meant to be all about *us.*

Such an idea borders on the kind of blasphemy that brings down lightning from heaven. We read of King Herod, "Immediately the angel of the Lord smote him, *because he gave not God the glory:* and he was eaten of worms, and gave up the ghost."[2]

The Bravehearted Gospel is serious stuff. It's all about making sure the glory ends up in the right place. I, for one, am not very interested in being smote by the angel of the Lord and eaten of worms. How about you? The bravehearted life is not a cool or hip version of living. It doesn't build a life that is in any way attractive to this world, approved by its leaders, or applauded by its masses. It is rather a "hidden" version of living.

As John the Baptist said when Jesus Christ arrived onto the scene, "He must increase, but I must decrease."[3] That is the gritty bravehearted pattern. It's diminishment of self, abandonment of rights, forsaking of worldly applause, and the foregoing of earthly comforts. All for the sake of Christ's glory!

The glory of God is not merely a side issue in the Bible. It is *the* issue. This whole creation thing all centers around it. And therefore, it is not something to toy around with (remember King Herod and the worms?).

The Bravehearted Gospel is all about forging a church that has ears to hear the angel crying out in Revelation 14:7, saying with a loud voice, "Fear God, and give glory to *him;* for the hour of his judgment is come: and worship *him* that made heaven, and earth, and the sea, and the fountains of waters."

Believe me, I am fully aware that the idea of making this life about something other than *me* doesn't sound too enjoyable. But ironically, the bravehearted life is the most thrilling life possible in this grand universe. I promise that it will certainly not fail you in the pleasure and enjoyment department. It just first has to shift what you consider to be pleasurable and enjoyable.

I am passionate about the glory of God. It moves me in everything I do. I think about it constantly. I am always aware of it, pondering it, esteeming it, desiring it, praying for it. The glory of God is all I really care about. In it I find my greatest delight, my greatest thrill, my greatest pleasure.

This burning desire for His glory drives me. And with the early Reformers I cry out the Latin term, "Soli Deo gloria!" ("to God *alone* be the glory!"). I lie awake at night pondering His glory, jealous for His reputation to be untarnished. I find myself deeply offended by Christians who cast slurs on His name, claiming Him to be calloused and unfeeling. I tremble with indignation when I hear Christian leaders speak of Jesus as some dude with a ponytail, a belly-button ring, and a goatee. For I ache deep within my soul to have this world see Jesus for who He truly is! I want the peoples of this Earth to behold the Lamb that was slain,[4] the Lion of the tribe of Judah,[5] the Majestic conqueror on the white steed with crowns on His head and a sword proceeding from His mouth.[6] And I am willing to do whatever it takes—to lay down any pleasure, and to take up any cross—to see the kingdom of my Jesus come.

That's not legalism. That's loyalty.

Part Seven

WHERE DO WE GO FROM HERE?

The practical potential of the Bravehearted Gospel

Twenty-seven

ENGRACED

Since legalism relies on human power to accomplish all its goals, its goals are usually quite smallish in stature. However, as you have surely come to see from reading this book, the pattern laid out in the Bravehearted Gospel is far beyond the strength, the aptitude, and the abilities of mere men to pull off. The call of this book is epic, grand, and majestic. And to be quite frank...*it's also impossible.*

If the bravehearted stuff is going to return, it isn't going to happen with raw grit and determination. It won't happen through intensive Bible reading, increased church attendance, and more consistent tithing. It won't happen by just talking about it, singing about it, or writing books about it. For the bravehearted stuff to return, the church needs good old-fashioned *grace.*

Unfortunately, the word *grace* has grown "girly" in our modern Christian world. It's gone soft and no longer packs any punch. Ask a modern-day Christian what grace is, and you are bound to hear a definition featuring such wonderful words as *mercy, kindness,* and *unmerited favor.* And whereas mercy, kindness, and unmerited favor are integral parts to the idea of grace, there is a muscular dimension, a manly dimension to the word that is strangely missing nowadays. Shocking, isn't it?

Grace has become a girl's name (note: the Greek word *charis* is a feminine noun, so I can't complain too much). No one who truly loved their son would ever consider naming him Grace. However, in my opinion, grace, if it is not a manly word, definitely has a manly side. For grace, when it is seen in its full-blown glory, is a thunderous, bravehearted, warrior-poet term.

Let's get some stuff out on the table about grace:

Grace is a lot more than maternal hugs and kisses for a world that has fallen and scraped its knee. There is also a gritty, growling side to grace that is powerful and strong. And this growling side of grace has large and painful splinters of wood in its palms and yet still reaches out its hands to serve, enduring the vast pain with extraordinary dignity. This growling side of grace has a muscular physique reminiscent of Hercules or Ulysses, but whereas these Greek heroes are mythical and forever chained to the dusty library of fiction, the muscle of the growling side of grace is real and living, ready to be spent on behalf of the saints of God. This growling side is smeared with streaks of blood. It's sweaty and heroic. It's brave, it's stouthearted, it's manly. This gritty side of grace is arduous and courageous work offered on behalf of another—to rescue them, to deliver them, to break the chains of their imprisonment, and to see them well fed and clothed for the rest of their life. This side of grace is serious commitment. It's serious expenditure. It is the giving of everything to someone who possesses nothing. Yes, grace is kind and merciful, but when you add back in the manly stuff, it is also so much more; it is God's power to perform God's tasks.

The word *grace* is very interesting in the Bible. In the Old Testament, the Hebrew word for grace is *chen*, which simply means "favor, acceptance, or charm." It's a rather innocuous word, denoting "special privilege, special notice, special attention, and unmerited blessing given from God to men." It is by no means a supremely powerful word in the Old Testament (there isn't a lot of blood and bravado mixed into it yet), but it is still, without a doubt, a significant concept, for it foreshadows things to come. It says, "There is One who will soon come who will embody this idea. He will be *Chen* [Grace] in human form. You will not deserve Him, but He will pay you special notice and give you special attentions nonetheless."

Jesus was grace, and still is grace. He was and is the undeserving gift of God. He was and is God giving special merciful attention to the rebels of earth (you and me), though it be completely undeserved. Jesus was and is the pathway bulldozed by the work of the cross by which one may finally be able to reach God.

The Old Testament merely sets the stage for grace in the New Testament. For it is in the New Testament that grace really takes off and earns its stripes, its medals, and its applause. In the book of Matthew, Jesus steps onto the scene and the vision of true grace begins to unfold before the entire nation of Israel. He was a man, but a man unlike any other, for He was also God. And though He was God, He chose to condescend to live *as a man,* to demonstrate how a man ought to live. And, as the grand story goes, He did this living *as a man* thing perfectly, without a spot of imperfection, without the smallest stumble, without a moment's hesitation whenever asked to obey. Jesus was tempted in every way that you and I are, but unlike us, He remained faultless and pure.

It says in the Bible, about Jesus, that He did nothing of His own strength or willpower. Everything He did, He did because the Father was doing it. He never spoke His own words; He spoke only what the Father was speaking. He never did His own good deeds; He did only the deeds that His Father was doing. He walked only where the Father was walking, healed only those whom the Father was healing, and even endured the cross because the Father said, "Pick up Your cross, My Son, and die!"

In other words, Jesus lived by grace.

If something about that last sentence sounds wrong to you, it is because we have associated grace for far too long with nothing but forgiveness and God's merciful willingness to overlook our *inabilities.* And of course, Jesus needed no forgiveness, and was able to do all things. So it sounds wrong to our modern Christian ear to say that Jesus lived by grace.

But rather than merely being God's kindly ignorance toward human weakness, grace in the New Testament is spoken of far more often as being God's power given to an individual to perform God's task. And Jesus, more than any man who has ever lived, had God's power and ability stamped all over everything He said and did.

"But Jesus was God," you might say.

Yes, that is true, but He came to earth *as a man;* He was tempted *as a man,* he overcame *as a man,* and He performed miraculous wonders and perfectly fulfilled the will of the Father *as a man!*

"Of mine own self *I can do nothing.*"[1] Jesus said things to this effect over and over again throughout His ministry so that we wouldn't miss it—so that we wouldn't be able to show up on the day of judgment with a Johnnie Cochran loophole, saying, "Well, the reason I didn't take up my cross and follow You is that I couldn't. I mean, sure, You lived that bravehearted life, and walked that bravehearted path, but *You* were God! Come on, I'm *just* a man. Give me a break! You can't expect me to live like You did!"

But not one sliver of this argument will hold water on that great and terrible day of the Lord, for Jesus lived His amazing life of glory and virtue not by some inbuilt, inbred divine power, but by the divine power of the heavenly Father as it was given and extended to Christ, the *Son of Man* moment by moment and miracle by miracle.

Jesus lived by grace.

And the same grace—the very same power that was given to Jesus by the Father to perform the Father's tasks—has been offered to you and me if we would only reach out, believe, and lay hold of it by faith. For salvation is *by* grace *through* faith.[2]

It is almost incomprehensible that the Creator of the universe, Jesus Christ, would confine Himself to such a place of utter dependence upon His Father and live a life of such humility and yieldedness. But, throughout this staggering picture of surrender and obedience, He was showcasing what grace is all about. He was demonstrating how you and I are supposed to live our lives—*entirely dependent upon God.* Jesus was God, yes, but He chose to live *as a man* in order to set a pattern for us to follow—*a pattern of grace.*

Let me explain:

Jesus demonstrated to humanity how the human life is supposed to look, work, and be. He said, "Watch Me!" And then He picked up His cross, looked over His shoulder, and said, "Now follow!" He literally asks us to follow Him in the direction of perfection.[3] Which sounds almost absurd, especially to all of us who have tried to live out perfect lives for Jesus and have failed miserably. We say, "Sure, *He* did this perfectly, but He was God! He needs to cut us a little slack!"

But this is where grace comes in. Jesus didn't just come to this Earth, live out to perfection the human life, command us to follow, then ditch us for the comforts of Heaven. He also made a way for us to follow. He provided everything we would need to walk in His footprints. *He gave us grace.*

But, contrary to popular opinion today, grace isn't just an accepting hug from God when we miserably fail in following Him. Rather, it is the power of God enabling us to follow so that we need not fail, but triumph.

Jesus was (and still is) the grace of God in the flesh, and when He departed Earth He promised that He would not leave us without also providing us with all the necessary equipment needed for life and godliness. So when He ascended to Heaven, He said (in paraphrase), "Wait! And soon I will send you everything you will need to pull off this impossible life!"

Jesus lived out to perfection the human life, showcasing God's intent for a man, exhibiting the glory of God in and through a man fully dependent on His life and grace. However, the reason grace is so amazing is that God desires to help us do the very same thing. No, we are not God, but the amazing news of the gospel is that God is saying, "Everything that I have is yours! Not just My forgiveness but My power, My virtue, and My strength! And if you will yield your body to become My temple, I will come and *I* will live through you all the beautiful realities of My nature and My kingdom!"

This is grace.

Peter wrote in his second epistle that God "according as his divine power hath given unto us all things that pertain unto life and godliness, through the knowledge of him that hath called us to glory and virtue." [4]

This is the special attention paid to us by God. This is the unmerited blessing bestowed upon humanity. It is without a doubt kind and merciful, but it is also powerful and energizing. He takes our miserably messed up lives and infuses them, according to *His* divine power, and transforms them into pictures of *His* love and *His* ability.

Paul is called the apostle of grace, so I assume that he knew a few things about grace. But Paul, in 2 Corinthians, doesn't emasculate God's grace to mean merely forgiveness for failure. Look at what he says: *"God is able* to make *all* grace *abound* toward you; that ye, *always* having *all* sufficiency in *all* good things, may *abound* to *every* good work." [5]

I'll tell you what! That doesn't seem to me to be a life that's barely getting by on the scraps of God's mercy! That definition of grace showcases the possibility of a life where *all* the power of God is *abounding, always,* in *all* sufficiency, in *all* things, within our souls, and filling us with *every* good work. No wonder Paul constantly exhorted the church to "grow in grace." There seems to be no end or limit to it!

How can you read that description of God's grace in 2 Corinthians and then go out and put a bumper sticker on the back of your car that says Christians are "*Just* forgiven"?

Just forgiven?

The power of almighty God has been purchased on our behalf, at the cost of the blood of God's own Son, and the only message we have to proclaim to the world is that we are *just* forgiven?

Did the cross of Christ really purchase so little?

Grace is the work of God on behalf of those who could never accomplish the task themselves. He did it and continues to do it for them. Grace is God's power to perform. Grace is the power of God given to men, enabling them to do things that otherwise would be impossible. It is God working in men to will and do His good pleasure. Grace is the life of God showcasing the love, joy, peace, patience, kindness, goodness, faithfulness, gentleness, and self-control *of God* in and through the surrendered human life. It is God living in us and showing the world what He actually looks like.

Like the entire construct of the Bravehearted Gospel, grace is the sweetest, most pleasant thing, as well as the most potent, powerful thing.

So what does it mean to be "saved by grace"? It means that we are saved by the work, effort, and Spirit-energy of God. He does the work on the cross that enables us to be inhabited by His presence, and then He continues to do the work in and through our lives, shaping us into a dynamic picture of His holiness. We are not *just* saved at the inception of our belief by grace. Rather, it is God's intent that we be "saved" by this grace every moment of every day of our lives moving forward. We need this grace not just for Heaven *but for Earth*. And not just for the beginning of the journey, but for the middle, and for the end, and for every occasion in between. Grace is the life of God imparted to us.

Contrary to what many of us might think, there are very few scriptures in the New Testament that utilize the idea of grace strictly in the "mercy and kindness" context. However, I *have* found over 20 verses that actually utilize the "power to perform" side without even mention of the "mercy and kindness" side. Here are a few that help enunciate this:

> By the grace of God I am what I am: and his grace which
> was bestowed upon me was not in vain; but I labored more

abundantly than they all: yet not I, but the grace of God which was with me.[6]

This is such an amazing picture of the grace of God working, laboring, and empowering.

With great power gave the apostles witness of the resurrection of the Lord Jesus: and great grace was upon them all.[7]

This isn't talking about great hugs being upon the apostles, but great empowerment.

Concerning his Son, Jesus Christ our Lord...by whom we have received grace and apostleship, for obedience to the faith among all nations, for his name.[8]

It appears that they received grace "for obedience":

According to the grace of God which is given unto me, as a wise masterbuilder, I have laid the foundation, and another buildeth thereon. But let every man take heed how he buildeth thereupon.[9]

Here grace is shown enabling Paul to lay a foundation.

The grace and gospel of Jesus Christ has been drained of its potency. It's been transformed into a message merely about the hugs and kisses of God, while the muscle and power of God is left standing on the sidelines wholly forgotten.

But God is in the business of building saints. He is the universe's foremost expert on overhauling the human existence and making it work the way it was originally intended to. And He does this overhaul with a tool known as *grace*. He saves us with it, He breaks us with it, He rebuilds us with it, and He fully equips us with it to turn this world upside down.

Grace is the life of Jesus imparted and living, moving, working, and thundering within our very bodies to accomplish the errands of God on planet Earth.

We are nothing without this grace. We can accomplish nothing without this grace. A book like this is an absolute joke if it is not put into action by the grace of God. The vision of the bravehearted life is merely a vision and can never become a vibrant reality unless the grace of God intersects our existence. We need this grace even more than we need air to breathe, water to drink, and food to eat. This is our life, literally.

The Bravehearted Gospel is not just another idea; it's historic Christianity. It's the way it has always been and must always continue to be.

It is a life that seeks not the applause of men, but rather, seeks the fame and renown of our King Jesus and is willing to stand alone, *contra mundum*, if need be, to remain loyal to His truth and to His person.

It is a life that is already dead. It has forsaken all the glitz and glamour of this world in order that it might find the pleasures of eternal communion with Jesus Christ. It is a life wholly spent on the things our great God deems most important. It is the life of a martyr—a living martyr.

It is a life fashioned after the heart of God. It esteems what God esteems, hates what God hates, embraces what God embraces, and fights that which God fights. It is a life hostile to the flesh and hospitable to the Spirit. And it is a life that gives no quarter to anything that proves hostile to the agenda of Christ both in the life of the individual and in the life of the church.

It is a life shaped after Scripture, testing and approving everything by the canon-tested Word of God. It's a life that is exclusive in its loyalties, heeding not the voices of anything contrary to the Budded Rod, Jesus Christ. It is a life fashioned after the canon-mind of the King of kings, the one who blossomed and bore almonds overnight in Jerusalem 2000 years ago.

It is a life fashioned and prepared for one single objective: to bring glory to the most high God. It is a life that forgets self and is consumed with the person of Christ. It is a life that jealously seeks the notoriety of the Lord of lords and will spend everything for the cause of turning people's hearts in His direction—if only they might see the glory of His countenance.

But how could such a life possibly be lived? How could you or I ever hope to bring the glory of such a life to bear once again upon this Earth?

The bravehearted life is built upon the simple premise: "I can't do it, but my God *can!*"

It is by *His* grace, *His* muscle, *His* life, and *His* enabling power alone that you or I could ever rise to such a glorious standard.

Only the life engraced can live out this impossible calling. And only the church engraced will cause this Earth to once again awaken to the grand and glorious realities found in the Bravehearted gospel of our King.

I know that the sheer vastness of this infinite type of grace can be hard to wrap your mind around. But I desperately want you—having come this far with me down the bravehearted path—to catch a soul-glimpse of the mighty power that fires the engines of this gritty gospel-driven life.

And so with Paul:

> For this cause I bow my knees unto the Father of our Lord Jesus Christ, of whom the whole family in heaven and earth is named, that he would grant you, according to the riches of his glory, to be strengthened with might by his Spirit in the inner man; that Christ may dwell in your hearts by faith; that ye, being rooted and grounded in love, may be able to comprehend with all saints what is the breadth, and length, and depth, and height; and to know the love of Christ, which passeth knowledge, that ye might be filled with all the fulness of God. Now unto him that is able to do exceeding abundantly above all that we ask or think, according to the power that worketh in us, unto him be glory in the church by Christ Jesus throughout all ages, world without end. Amen.
>
> Ephesians 3:14-21

THE
BRAVEHEARTED
PATH

EPILOGUE

This book by no means is the final statement on the bravehearted way of life. In fact, it barely has scratched the surface. Unfortunately, the idea of the bravehearted life is far too big of a concept for one singular book. Unless, that is, the book being written were trying to be the next *War and Peace*. But truth these days has to be more bite-sized—otherwise, it seems that it is missed altogether. So, for the sake of trying to make this volume a bit more approachable and digestible, quite a few exciting dimensions of the bravehearted life have been forced to stand on the sidelines and sit this particular book out. So let me give you a quick overview of what you are missing. Basically, this is the "if I had another 300 pages" summary:

Nobility and honor—this is one of my favorite ideas, but I just couldn't figure out how to fit this in without distracting from the heart of the message. When the manly stuff enters back into the faith, then accompanying it is a sense of regal decorum and dignity. Men become gentlemen and women become ladies. But this idea goes far beyond a Jane Austen novel; this is the kingdom of Heaven in full-blown wonder unveiled on planet Earth. It is Mr. Knightly meets William Wallace; it's beauty and poetry meets sword and standard.

Operation least—this is one of my great passions in life—to practically assist the little children in need: the orphans, the street children, the child prostitutes, the child soldiers, and the child slaves. This is a leading idea in the bravehearted playbook, and as you probably noticed,

I did find small ways to stick this idea into the text. But this idea has a lot more meat on it that a true braveheart is definitely going to want to understand.

Exposing the moles and marking the saboteurs—this aspect of the brave-hearted life is definitely hard for many modern Christians to swallow. This book was probably already challenging enough as is without bring-ing in this additional weight. But its exclusion should by no means be construed as a diminishment of its importance. There are many wolves running free inside the sheep pen of Christianity these days. And it takes the bravehearted stuff to stand up and point them out. Paul the apostle warns us to mark these men and avoid them.

The manly voice of preaching re-inaugurated—preaching is different than teaching. Preaching is a form of communication that somehow speaks to the spirit of a man and not just the mind. It stirs a soul, con-victs it, and endues a grace into it that enables it to see and believe. But preaching offends this world, and even offends the church. It seems too abrasive and unfeeling, and to be honest, quite foolish. But Paul says that God deliberately has chosen "the foolishness of preaching to save them that believe."[1] Historically, it has always been through wrestling prayer and Spirit-born preaching that the fires of revival have been started. So whether we like it or not, we need the manly voice of preaching re-inaugurated.

Wrestling prayer—this topic demands an entire book all to itself. You see, wrestling prayer is different than dinner prayer. Wrestling prayer is the violent and aggressive taking of enemy territory in and through the process of prayer. It is waiting on God for specific prayer objectives and then laboring in prayer until those objectives are gained. It is tireless, throughout-the-night, persistent praying. And when wrestling prayer returns to the church, Hell will tremble!

Manly tears—this might not seem like something that would be associated with the manly stuff, but it is. And it involves the very uncomfortable process of implanting God's heart inside of our chests and causing us to supernaturally feel precisely what He feels. And let me forewarn you, this is severe pain. But it is the necessary pain of love. William Booth, the great revivalist preacher, when asked how to gain a mighty move of God within a community, said, "Try tears!"[2]

The awakening to the reality of Hell—that same William Booth, just mentioned, was once quoted as saying that if he could do it, he would have finalized the training of his disciples by having them hang for 24 hours over Hell, so they could see its eternal torment.³ What a miserable 24 hours those would be! But just imagine what would be gained through it! No longer could we sit idle while countless millions are dying and going there without as much as a bead of perspiration on our part. When we as the church are once again awakened to the reality of Hell, we are awakened to the desperate reality of the destiny of the souls about us.

If this book could have handled it, then I probably would have made you even more uncomfortable than you already are. So you can thank the sound-bite nature of our modern culture for sparing you. But even after these above-mentioned dimensions of the bravehearted life, there are probably 20 more besides that are in need of being brought back to the center stage of Christian life and thought today.

Will it be uncomfortable to do this? I think you know the answer to that one.

I'm perfectly confident that there is an army of soldiers out there that is simply looking for the right battle for which to enlist. I hope after reading this book, you've found your battle.

If you are interested in participating in the emergence of a revitalized historic Christianity that will shape and impact Christian faith for the next 100 years, then please contact us. The bravehearted community is not a stagnate one. We are not a Sunday morning-Wednesday night sort of crowd. We are an all-day, everyday rendition of radical faith and practice.

If you are looking for spiritual employment, please speak with us. We are organizing, even as you read this, to practically assist the North American church in rescuing the orphan, the street children, the child prostitutes, the child soldiers, and the child slaves. We want to train up an army of believers who will be willing to risk all to see the authority of Scripture defended, the name of God glorified, and the spit wiped off the face of Christ. And we need frontline men and women who don't consider their lives as more important than the gospel of Jesus Christ.

If this book touched a nerve in your soul and you are begging to take it deeper, then please seek out our web site. If you are one who desires to live out the Bravehearted Gospel, then please consider joining us for one of our upcoming conferences or events.

The manly stuff is needed. But who will bring it back to the church? Could it be that it is supposed to be you?

www.TheBraveheartedGospel.com

Chapter 2

1. Job 1:7-8.
2. Job 1:21.
3. The King James Version reads "eschewed evil."
4. Matthew 10:32.
5. There is an argument that could be made that Noah should be included in this short list based on Genesis 6:9. However, this might just be referring to his genetic purity (not being mixed with the seed of angels) and not necessarily referencing Noah's moral purity.

Chapter 4

1. Matthew chapter 23.
2. Blind is used to describe the Pharisees five times in Matthew 23.
3. Matthew 23:33.
4. Matthew 23:33.
5. Matthew 23:15.

Chapter 5

1. Acts 5:3.
2. 2 Timothy 3:12.
3. My wife's book *Set-Apart Femininity: the Blueprint for World-altering Femininity* (Eugene, OR: Harvest House Publishers, 2008) is an excellent resource for anyone interested in pursuing this theme further.

The Bravehearted Path—Where it begins

1. A.W. Tozer, *Of God and Men* (Harrisburg, PA: Christian Publications, 1960), pp. 15-16.

Chapter 8

1. Matthew 18:16-17.
2. 1 Corinthians 5:1-5, emphasis added.

Chapter 9

1. For instance, one of the leading churches in America today ranks their pastor's favorite 100 beers on the church's Web site.

Chapter 12

1. 1 Corinthians 1:27-28.
2. John 1:46.
3. Matthew 16:24.
4. Luke 17:33.
5. Accessed at www.Christianpost.com, http://www.christianpost.com/article/20070605/27804_The_Danger_of_World-Worship.htm.
6. Revelation 19.

The Bravehearted Path—Contra Mundum

1. Dave Hunt, *What Love Is This?* (Sisters, OR: Loyal Publishing, 2002), pp. 165-78.
2. Leonard Ravenhill, *Why Revival Tarries* (Minneapolis: Bethany House, 1959), p. 76.
3. Accessed at http://theodsseyblogger.typepad.com/theodyssey/2007/05/athanasius_cont.html.
4. Greg. Naz. Or. XXI (trans. by Browne and Swallow), in *The Nicene and Post-Nicene Fathers*, vol. VII.
5. Ravenhill, *Why Revival Tarries*, p. 76.
6. Dr. Jack L. Arnold, "Luther and Melanchthon: Reformation Men and Theology," Lesson 5 of 11, *IIIM Magazine Online*, vol. 1, no. 5, March 29 to April 4, 1999.
7. James 4:4.

Chapter 13

1. Brian McLaren, the father of the emergent church, has an entire chapter on this, entitled "Why I Am Green" in his book *A Generous Orthodoxy* (Grand Rapids: Zondervan, 2006).
2. If you wish to know more about our "historic emergent" ministries, please visit us at www.TheStoneMountainProject.com.

Chapter 14

1. Rob Bell, *Velvet Elvis* (Grand Rapids: Zondervan, 2005), pp. 22,27.
2. Rob Bell, *Velvet Elvis*, pp. 27-28.
3. 2 Samuel 22:47; Psalm 62:7; Matthew 7:24-25;16:18; Luke 6:48; Romans 9:33; 1 Corinthians 3:11; 10:4; 1 Peter 2:8; Isaiah 26:4
4. Hebrews 13:8; 1 Peter 2:6.

Chapter 15

1. *King Lear*, Act 3.
2. This is the port from which Columbus launched his great journey.
3. 2 Corinthians 6:14-17.
4. John 14:6.
5. 2 Corinthians 10:5.

Chapter 16

1. Matthew 7:15; Acts 17:10-11.
2. Matthew 7:15.

Chapter 17

1. Romans 8:37.
2. Mike Yaconelli, *Messy Spirituality* (Grand Rapids: Zondervan, 2002), pp. 10-11.

Chapter 18

1. Genesis 32:25-28.
2. Here are some illuminating scriptures about the corrosive nature of doubt: Matthew 13:58; 21:21; Mark 16:14; Acts 10:20; 11:12; Romans 4:20; 11:20; 14:23; James 1:6; Hebrews 3:12,19.

Chapter 19

1. Gary Wolf, "The New Atheist," *Wired,* Nov. 2006, p. 184.
2. Ibid., p. 191.

3. Philip Yancey, *Reaching for the Invisible God* (Grand Rapids: Zondervan, 2000), p. 18.
4. Ibid., p. 41.
5. Ibid., p. 21.
6. E.M. Bounds, *The Complete Works on E.M. Bounds on Prayer* (Grand Rapids: Family Christian Press, 1990), p. 20.

Chapter 20

1. Accessed at http://christianpost.com/article/20060112/13940_U.S._Church_leaders Youth_Ministers_Address_Christian_Youth_Fallout.htm.
2. Philip Yancey refers to Gandhi as one of 13 spiritual directors who have most shaped his life and thought (see Yancey's book entitled *Soul Survivor* [New York: Doubleday, 2001]).

The Bravehearted Path—Living Martyrs

1. Josef Ton, *Suffering, Martyrdom and Rewards in Heaven* (Wheaton, IL : The Romanian Missionary Society, 2000), p. 339.
2. Deuteronomy 1:21.
3. Matthew 7:14.
4. *Foxe's Book of Martyrs* see at http://exclassics.com/foxe/foxe4.htm.
5. See the entire book of Philippians.

Chapter 21

1. 2 Timothy 2:15.
2. Rob Bell, *Velvet Elvis* (Grand Rapids: Zondervan, 2005), p. 53.
3. Genesis 3:1.

Chapter 23

1. McLaren unlocks this idea on page 185 of his popular book *A Generous Orthodoxy* (Grand Rapids: Zondervan, 2004).
2. Rob Bell, *Velvet Elvis* (Grand Rapids: Zondervan, 2005), pp. 62,50,46.
3. 2 Peter 1:20-21.
4. See page 189 of McLaren's *A Generous Orthodoxy*.
5. McLaren utilizes this idea throughout his book, *A Generous Orthodoxy*, though never states it clearly. He simply believes that to fulfill the purposes of God on planet Earth, truth *adapts* to each culture in order to express the kindness, love, and mercy of God.
6. Hebrews 13:8.
7. James 1:17.
8. Leonard Ravenhill, *Why Revival Tarries* (Minneapolis: Bethany House, 1959), p. 15.
9. Flavius Josephus, *Against Apion,* Book 1, Section 8, p. 158.
10. Revelation 22:18-19.
11. Adapted from Samuel Davidson, *The Hebrew Text of the Old Testament,* 2nd ed., p. 89, as cited in James Hastings, ed., *A Dictionary of the Bible,* vol. IV (New York: Charles Scribner's Sons, 1923), p. 949.
12. Wheeler Robinson, ed. *The Bible in Its Ancient and English Versions* (London: Oxford University Press, 1940), pg. 29. This is also detailed at http://www.appiusforum.com/biblioOT.html.
13. Matthew 5:18.

The Bravehearted Path—The Canon-minded

1. Ezekiel 40:2-4; Revelation 11:1.
2. Ezekiel 20:37; Proverbs 13:24; 22:15.

3. Psalm 23:4.

4. Psalm 110:2; Micah 6:9; Revelation 19:15.

5. 2 Timothy 3:16.

6. 2 Timothy 3:16-17.

7. Ecclesiastes 8:4.

8. Numbers 16.

9. John 1:1.

10. Psalm 2:6-9 (evidenced in Luke 1:30-35).

11. Genesis 3:14-15 (evidenced in Galatians 4:4).

12. Genesis 17:7-8 (evidenced in Galatians 3:16).

13. Genesis 21:12 (evidenced in Hebrews 11:17-19).

14. Psalm 132:11 (evidenced in Acts 13:21-23; Romans 1:1-4).

15. Isaiah 7:14 (evidenced in Luke 2:7; Matthew 1:18-23).

16. Micah 5:2 (evidenced in Matthew 2:1; Luke 2:4-6).

17. Psalm 72:10-11 (evidenced in Matthew 2:1-11).

18. Hosea 11:1 (evidenced in Matthew 2:13-15).

19. Isaiah 40:3; Malachi 3:1; 4:5 (evidenced in Matthew 3:1-3; 11:9-15; 17:10-12).

20. Psalm 45:7 (evidenced in Matthew 3:16).

21. Isaiah 9:1-2 (evidenced in Matthew 4:12-19).

22. Zechariah 9:9 (evidenced in Matthew 21:1-5).

23. Isaiah 53:1-2 (evidenced in Mark 6:3).

24. Isaiah 42:1-3 (evidenced in Matthew 12:14).

25. Isaiah 53:9 (evidenced in 1 Peter 2:21-25).

26. Psalm 69:9 (evidenced in John 2:13-22).

27. Psalm 22 (evidenced in Romans 15:3).

28. Psalm 41:9 (evidenced in John 13:18-19).

29. Zechariah 13:7 (evidenced in Matthew 26:31,56).

30. Zechariah 11:12-13 (evidenced in Matthew 26:15;27:3).

31. Isaiah 53:12 (evidenced in Matthew 15:27-30).

32. Isaiah 53:12 (evidenced in Luke 23:34).

33. Isaiah 53:12 (evidenced in Matthew 27:50-54).

34. Exodus 12:46; Psalm 34:20 (evidenced in John 19:33-36).

35. Zechariah 12:10 (evidenced in John 19:34).

36. Psalm 22:18 (evidenced in John 19:24).

37. Psalm 16:10 (evidenced in Luke 24:6-8).

38. Psalm 68:18 (evidenced in Luke 24: 51-53).

39. Psalm 110:1 (evidenced in Hebrews 1:3).

40. Genesis 14:18 (evidenced in Hebrews 7:15-17).

41. Isaiah 4:1-6; 11:1-5; Jeremiah 23:5-6; 33:14-18; Zechariah 3:1-9; 6:9-13.

Chapter 24

1. I have had this stated to me as originating from Charles Finney, which I have been unable to confirm. But, no matter the origin of the statement, I concur with a hearty amen.

Chapter 25

1. Leonard Ravenhill, *Why Revival Tarries* (Minneapolis: Bethany House, 1959), p. 106.
2. Leonard Ravenhill, as cited at http://www.godcentered.info/2007.10.24WED.Revival.Hymn.pdf.
3. Philippians 1:21.

Chapter 26

1. Leonard Ravenhill, *Why Revival Tarries* (Minneapolis: Bethany House, 1959), p. 100.
2. 1 Corinthians 6:9-10, emphasis added.
3. James 2:20.

The Bravehearted Path—Soli Deo gloria

1. Harper Grace Ludy arrived home July 18, 2007. She is indescribably precious. You can see pictures on www.setapartlife.com.
2. Acts 12:23.
3. John 3:30.
4. Revelation 5:12.
5. Revelation 5:5.
6. Revelation 19:11-16.

Chapter 27

1. John 5:30.
2. Ephesians 2:8.
3. Matthew 5:48.
4. 2 Peter 1:3.
5. 2 Corinthians 9:8, emphasis added.
6. 1 Corinthians 15:10.
7. Acts 4:33.
8. Romans 1:3,5.
9. 1 Corinthians 3:10.

The Bravehearted Path—Epilogue

1. 1 Corinthians 1:21.
2. Leonard Ravenhill, *Why Revival Tarries* (Minneapolis: Bethany House, 1959), p. 53.
3. Ibid., p.33.

Wondering where to go from here?
take the next step...

The Truth Is Worth Fighting For

THE
BRAVEHEARTED
GOSPEL

ERIC LUDY

The battle of the ages is
about to begin.

Death and life hang in
the balance for millions.

You can
make a difference.

www.thebraveheartedgospel.com
will show you how.

Throughout the centuries the true church of Jesus Christ has emerged out of war, culture, persecution, religion, apostasy and error. Today the true Church is emerging once again. Out of the ashes of dead religion, a struggle has been born between truth and deception that will alter the Church forever. By God's grace we intend to do everything in our power to see that living, vibrant and relevant historic Christianity rise from this conflict as the emergent victor to represent Jesus Christ for the next century and beyond with passion, love, honor and power. We invite you to join us - not in a conversation, not in a dialogue or a movement, but as a soldier of Jesus Christ in the battle of the ages. You can help change the world...

Maybe one last time